SACRED GROUND

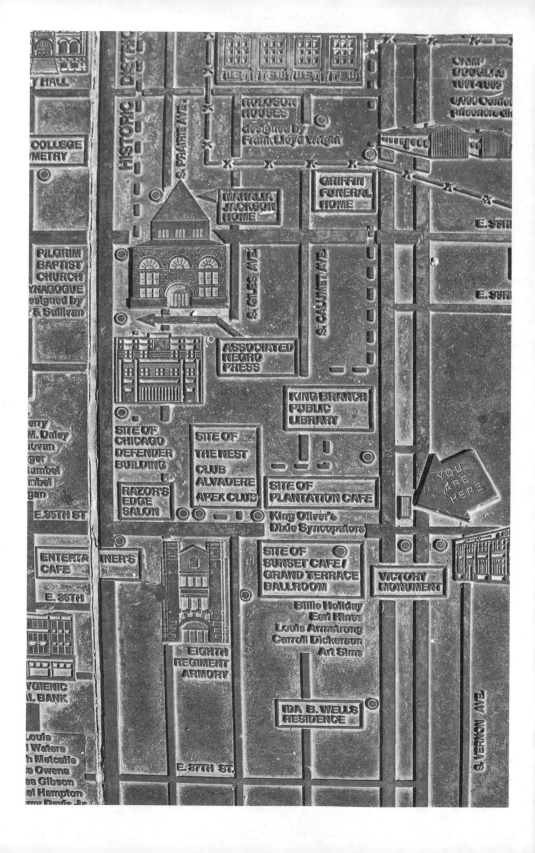

SACRED GROUND

{
THE CHICAGO STREETS OF TIMUEL BLACK
}

TIMUEL D. BLACK JR.

As told to Susan Klonsky

Edited by Bart Schultz

NORTHWESTERN UNIVERSITY PRESS
EVANSTON, ILLINOIS

Northwestern University Press
www.nupress.northwestern.edu

All photographs courtesy of the author unless otherwise noted.

Frontispiece: A section of the bronze street map at Thirty-Fifth Street and
Dr. Martin Luther King Jr. Drive; photograph by Bart Schultz.

Printed in the United States of America

10   9   8   7   6   5   4   3   2   1

Library of Congress Cataloging-in-Publication Data

Names: Black, Timuel D., Jr., author. | Klonsky, Susan, author. | Schultz,
   Bart, editor.
Title: Sacred ground : the Chicago streets of Timuel Black / Timuel D. Black Jr.
   as told to Susan Klonsky ; edited by Bart Schultz.
Description: Northwestern University Press : Evanston, 2019. | Includes index.
Identifiers: LCCN 2018036763| ISBN 9780810139244 (pbk. : alk. pa-
   per) | ISBN 9780810139251 (ebook)
Subjects: LCSH: Black, Timuel D., Jr. | Civil rights workers—United States—
   Biography. | African Americans—Illinois—Chicago—Biography. | Rac-
   ism—United States—History—20th century. | Chicago (Ill.)—Race
   relations. | Chicago (Ill.)—Social conditions—20th century. | Chicago
   (Ill.)—Social life and customs—20th century.
Classification: LCC F548.9.N4 .B558 2018 | DDC 977.311004960730092—
   dc23
LC record available at https://lccn.loc.gov/2018036763

For Mama and Daddy, my uncles and aunts, and all of my family, friends, and companions who helped shape my experiences on what I now call Sacred Ground

Mem'ries light the corners of my mind
Misty water-colored mem'ries of the way we were
Scattered pictures of the smiles we left behind
Smiles we gave to one another for the way we were

> —"The Way We Were," written by Alan Bergman,
> Marilyn Bergman, and Marvin Hamlisch

Even when I listen to a popular song such as "The Way We Were" as it was interpreted by Gladys Knight, I hear not only the voice of the singer herself but also our voices—the voices of all the people I knew and still know—and now I want to share those voices with you and also with your children's children so that they will be able to hear what I heard and know what once was known not only to me but to an entire community as well.

> —TIMUEL D. BLACK, *Bridges of Memory: Chicago's First Wave of Black Migration*

Contents

Galley follows page 88.

Acknowledgments

For making this book possible, I would like to thank my wife of over thirty years, Zenobia Johnson Black, my daughter, Ermetra Black Thomas, and all the old friends who shared their reflections specifically for this book, including Bill Daniels, Steve Saltzman, Clarice Durham, and Leon Decosta Dash. I wish that space had allowed us to include more of their reflections, and those of Elisabeth Todd-Breland, Adam Green, and all the other talented young scholars who have honored me with their commentary. Maybe the third volume of *Bridges of Memory* will be able to say more about them. Also, my sincerest thanks to the dedicated editors at Northwestern University Press, Mike Levine, Gianna Mosser, Jill Petty, and Anne Gendler, who had to push so hard to bring the project to completion. Susan Klonsky and Bart Schultz pulled everything together in the end, with some help from Christopher Reed, Mike Drapa, and Esha Mishra, an intern with the University of Chicago Civic Knowledge Project who recorded an audio version for me to review. Thanks also to the DuSable Museum of African American History. Of course, my biggest debt is to all the people and places that made up my Sacred Ground. My story is our story, and it is an American story, for people of color in the United States.

SACRED GROUND

Introduction:
A Reasonable Assumption

All four of my grandparents were slaves. I am the grandson and the great-grandson of slaves on both sides—my mama's and my daddy's parents and all of my great-grandparents labored first as slaves and later as sharecroppers on Alabama cotton plantations. That is why I believe I am descended from the best and the brightest. This seems to me a perfectly reasonable assumption.

After all, think about what you do when you go shopping. You look for the best product you can buy at the lowest price. What do you think the slave traders did? They kidnapped and sold the best physical specimens they could find, the strongest and the most beautiful, as well as the most skilled craftsmen, the finest musicians—the best they could find. They found well-built girls and women too, who looked like they were tough enough both to survive toil in the fields and to maximize the slave owners' investment by bearing children—generations of slaves from one initial purchase.

I always make this point when I speak to young people at schools, and as an educator, I do a lot of that. Society has taught our black children to look down upon themselves, to lack pride in their heritage. I want them to know that even when we were slaves, we were selected for our power, our skill, our strength, and our intelligence. Even when we were debased, they picked us because we were the best of the best.

During the seventeenth century, after the slave trade arose in Europe and took force in the New World, the African black slaves were treated as simple heathens who needed to be Christianized. However, the internal resources, intellectual power, and physical endurance of the slaves permitted them not merely to survive, but to develop a new culture upon the foundation of their old African cultures. That new culture has spread across the globe right up until today. The slaves retained part of their own culture and injected it into the Christianity that was imposed upon them. This new, hybrid culture is best illustrated by their Christian music—the spirituals and ultimately, gospel music—out of which emerged, eventually, blues and jazz and even today's hip-hop, influencing musicians both black and white. You don't think of it as rooted in slave culture, but when I listen, I hear the echoes. I hear the voices, the calls and responses of our ancestors' rhythmic labor chopping the cotton and pulling the plow and cutting the cane. The rhythms are universal and still with us.

Some of my life story in this book is about my family, and some is about my community and my people, but mostly I hope it is a human story, about how human beings treat each other and how people struggle to reach higher ground.

My world outlook was shaped by my parents' long view of history. My parents lived in Alabama, and they knew many elders who had been slaves—not only their own parents and grandparents, but the parents of their contemporaries. Perhaps this gave my parents some perspective. They could see how we had progressed from slavery; they wanted us children to understand that you don't quit simply because things aren't where you want them to be right now. They moved to Chicago and kept on pushing. It was their hopes and dreams that kept them and kept us—and still keep us—alive. That's not racial. Any and every oppressed group has done this—pushing, persisting, and preserving their cultures. Take the Jews in the Warsaw ghetto: they documented their fight to survive through buried milk cans full of photographs, clandestine film, letters smuggled out, and really any means at hand, and they took up arms in the resistance. There are many ways to struggle. But you don't ever give up. From what I've seen in this world, I find that resistance to oppression is a universal. It is the ultimate human trait.

A family story has it that when I was just eight months old, I looked around at the oppression in Birmingham, Alabama, where I was born, and said, "Shit, I'm leaving here." My mama said to my daddy, "Dixie, that boy can't even change his diapers—we'd better go with him." The story is humorous but has a serious point. My family knew we were not safe in Birmingham, especially since my daddy—everyone called him "Dixie"—did not put up with any nonsense. So, when I was less than one year old, my parents came to Chicago from Alabama. My sister, Charlotte, was ten years old, and my brother, Walter, was four years old.

I was the baby. My parents arrived in Chicago with quite a handful—their worldly possessions plus the three of us. We came by train, like tens of thousands of Alabama blacks who came north in the first Great Migration. This was in the summer of 1919, the summer of the Chicago race riot.

We arrived in August 1919, mere weeks after the riot. Some two dozen black Chicagoans had died at the hands of white mobs, who raced through the few black neighborhoods of the city setting fires, beating, and murdering. The mayhem was sparked by the murder of a black teenager, Eugene Williams, who was stoned to death after he unwittingly crossed the line separating the black from the white swimming areas at the beach on Lake Michigan by Twenty-Ninth Street. But it was the culmination of worsening competition for jobs in the stockyards, the packing plants, and the mills when the white soldiers returned after World War I. Ethnic European immigrants sought to defend their perceived interests against us, the newcomers. But even knowing about the fresh Chicago violence, my parents were among the tens of thousands who came north anyway. Perhaps they viewed the race riot as an aberration, whereas the white terror that constantly threatened in Alabama was a permanent feature. I am not sure. But after that week of violence, black Chicago knew it would have to build its own community, without help from white Chicago.

The first Great Migration was encouraged by the *Chicago Defender*, the flagship black newspaper disseminated throughout the South by the black railway employees. It was said that every copy of the *Defender* changed hands at least five times. Its editor and publisher, Robert Sengstacke Abbott, exhorted southern blacks to come north for opportunity, particularly to jobs in the Chicago stockyards, on the railroad, and in the mills. He was unabashed in his appeal to blacks to take jobs as "replacement workers" when labor struggles resulted in mass firings of strikers. In the fast-growing industrial economy, Abbott promised, you might start on the bottom, but with a little effort you would rise. His newspaper was peppered with success stories about black entrepreneurs who had arrived with little in the way of capital, but who in Chicago had built churches, hotels, insurance companies, funeral homes, and cosmetics companies and other specialty businesses catering to black consumers. In a burgeoning, segregated market, one had only to hang out a shingle and a black dentist or beautician had a guaranteed clientele at the door.

A tiny neighborhood grocery store didn't require much money to get started, but it could feed an extended family for generations, and I still know South Side families who started with a fruit stand the day they got off the train.

I have told this story hundreds of times, how we were welcomed to the big city. We got off the train at the Twelfth Street Station and were met by relatives and friends who coached my parents about how you live in a city: *Don't spit on the sidewalk. Don't walk on the grass. Don't talk too loud. If you're reading the Defender, put it inside the Tribune.* Although my parents were urbanized folk from Birmingham, life was so different in the North. We members of the first Great Migration from the South—my parents' and my generation—received this training from the black friends and relatives who were already in the North. Jewish immigrants were instructed by their relatives not to behave like "greenhorns"— naive new arrivals. Black immigrants were instructed how not to behave "country"—ignorant of city ways. I imagine that every generation of immigrants from anywhere receives similar instruction on how to assimilate, how to blend in, how to become successful.

The training was profound, as well as intrusive and judgmental. It carried within it the weight of hard-learned lessons. *Don't have too many babies. You're not down south anymore.* In the urban South as in the North, babies cost money. But in the rural South, babies were an asset. You needed more hands to work the farm, to feed the family. Isn't it still the case today? In modern China, the government for several decades imposed an across-the-board limit of one child per family, and it was the farm people who most sharply opposed this rule, now cast aside. This is a social habit that transcends race. In Chicago, when we would see a woman with several small children and perhaps another on the way, my mother would cluck with disapproval, raise her eyebrows, and ask aloud, "How they gon' pay for 'em?" In strictly segregated Chicago, where housing for blacks was at a premium, this was a question with real practical impact. We were densely packed into such a small area, and we observed each other closely and critically.

Sometimes things get so singularly racial that people can't see that it's just human behavior. This is not just an American phenomenon. Minorities are excluded from the mainstream. They can be and are used as an instrument of capitalism. You can see it in Africa. In South Africa, there is still tremendous poverty, but we also have seen the recent rise

of a class of African leaders who form a new elite, while the poor people are not much better off economically than they were before the defeat of the apartheid system. Indeed, behaviorally speaking, the new elites are very much like those who were at the top layers of the apartheid system. It's true here, and it's true over there. It's part of that human story, about how human beings treat each other.

My own story is part of that human story, too, and it is in many ways a fairly ordinary immigration story. How we were educated and how we lived through war and upheaval and the Great Depression and the movement for justice. Throughout this book I will whenever possible name the street and the block where we lived, the locations of our schools and theaters, our churches, the parks, and the other sites where the story unfolds. For I do view it as Sacred Ground, and to me, it has a precise and eternal locale. For me, to this day, that particular neighborhood of Chicago is my Sacred Ground. It has been called the "Black Belt," the "Black Metropolis," and, because of James Gentry, an editor for the old *Chicago Bee*—another one of the black newspapers on the South Side—"Bronzeville," meant as an expression of pride. It lies from Twenty-Sixth Street on the north to Sixty-Third on the south, and from Cottage Grove on the east to State Street on the west. I can walk from where I live now, at Forty-Ninth and Drexel Boulevard, to every house where I ever lived. When I walk those streets I can stop and look at the buildings where we lived. I can remember faces, voices, melodies from my loved ones on these streets.

I am lucky to still have a few friends around the neighborhood who go all the way back to our childhoods together. One of my classmates from Edmund Burke Elementary School is Velda Hines, a former social worker who is now ninety-seven years of age. Her folks had a small business in the black ghetto, a grocery store. Another friend I've had since the age of seven or eight is Norman Burrell, who also attended Burke Elementary. Norm recently lost both his legs, but he is alert, aware, and politically active. Whenever we talk, we still recall not just the battles we've been through, but all the fun we had on this Sacred Ground. And we remember all the friends who are no longer with us, people like William "Billy Boy" Green, who went on to become the first black agent for the Internal Revenue Service, and Carl Cotton, who became a taxidermist at the Field Museum, possibly the first black to hold such a position. There was Cleophas "Tally Ho" Smith, Carl "Carlos the Cool" Caldwell,

Lonnie Young, Bob Carroll, and so many others. Their stories are part of my story and all of us are part of the story of this Sacred Ground.

For me, this expression—Sacred Ground—is not a cliché, but a real, hallowed space, from which major figures in the freedom movement emerged, and where historic commitments were forged. Some of the names of those freedom fighters are well known. Others were the unnamed rank-and-file of the freedom movement and of the labor movement born in Chicago.

Understand that our family moved not simply to Chicago, but specifically and intentionally to the *South Side* of Chicago. This was the main area where black folks could live and could find housing. Our first residence was on the 4900 block of St. Lawrence Avenue. When we got there in 1919, the neighborhood was predominantly white, but those whites soon ran off. And from then on, it became an expanding black community.

Now I am ninety-nine years of age. I have lived here in the same neighborhood continuously, except for a few brief interludes in other cities and during World War II. I have walked the streets of this neighborhood since 1919. So I want to talk about *this* Sacred Ground. It's a real place. It's still here. We have overcome a lot, and there's still plenty of overcoming to be done.

In our own ways, each of us, the early migrants and their children, are sustained by a spiritual sensibility, captured so well by the great Duke Ellington in his lyric "Come Sunday," from his first Sacred Concert. I've been reciting this lyric to myself for many, many years whenever I need a lift.

> Lord, dear Lord above, God almighty,
> God of love, please look down and see my people through.
> I believe that God put sun and moon up in the sky.
> I don't mind the gray skies
> 'cause they're just clouds passing by.

Duke Ellington was above all a humanist, a spiritual composer. People don't think of Duke Ellington as political, but he distilled with that lyric the notion that *we can overcome.* As a young man, I took inspiration and encouragement perhaps more from song lyrics like Duke's than from Bible study. We have always taken sustenance from the words that remind us we are meant for something better.

My full name is Timuel Dixon Black Jr. My mama selected Timuel, also my daddy's first name, because she thought it sounded biblical. She told me it meant I am a child of God. My father's first name was Timuel, but his middle name was also Dixon, and again, he was known as Dixie. Norm still calls me "TD." He thinks he's the only one who still knows my nickname. By the 1960s, some characters referred to me as "TDB." *Too Damn Black*. TDB. They didn't necessarily mean it as a compliment. But I chose to take it as one.

When I thought about writing this book, I thought there must be something of wider value in my stories. I worried that this book might seem vain or egotistical. The fact is, I don't give a damn about Tim Black as some sort of shining light. I consider my story to be fairly *typical* of men and women of my generation. I believe my life is fairly representative of the lives of many of the children of migrants from the Deep South. My story's *typical* ness is precisely where its value lies. What might be learned from our stories? Considering where we started, how did we get over—or not get over—coming up the way we did? Sometimes it amazes me, even now.

As I will explain, we grew up in the midst of the Great Depression. At my daddy's income level, we should have been on welfare. But my daddy's point of view was, "We'll starve to death before we go on relief." He wasn't joking. He would go door to door in Hyde Park offering to wash windows or cut grass, but he wouldn't go on welfare. Velda's and Norm's families had income. Norm's father worked in one of the downtown hotels, and most of the children of the black hotel employees went on to college. But for all of us, including my mama and daddy, education was a top priority, and I'll be saying a lot about that in the pages that follow. Education is a big part of this story, and of my story.

After all, teaching has defined much of my adult life. I taught in high schools, colleges, and universities. Among my students there were some remarkable individuals. In this book, I'll tell you about a few of them.

I think often of my student Bill Daniels. Bill graduated from my own alma mater, DuSable High School, in 1956. Bill was a ward of the state and a foster child. Nowadays they would classify him as "at risk."

"William," said his guidance counselor, "you didn't do very well on the test. I think you ought to keep that job you have at Sears Roebuck." In other words, you are meant to be a stock boy. Not "college material." I visited all of my homeroom students at their homes. Bill told me what his guidance counselor had said. I told him, "William, she can't tell you what you can do. Only *you* can tell you what you can do." The administrators and other teachers didn't recognize Bill's other qualities: he was an outstanding swimmer, he was on the chess team, he was good-looking, he was diplomatic, and he was a good student. He just didn't do well on tests. He had outlined where he wanted to be. I got in touch with the Pullman Foundation, and we got him a scholarship to go to college. Off he went to Upper Iowa University, where he was the second black student ever. I took him over from Chicago and kept in touch with him throughout his college years. He graduated Phi Beta Kappa. Bill's story, like many of the others related in this book, figures in my volumes of oral history, *Bridges of Memory*.

Similarly, there was the brilliant young Ron Gault. He too attended DuSable and went off to college. Ron became an international development banker. He is married to the journalist and civil rights leader Charlayne Hunter-Gault. Ron still calls me from South Africa. They are the children of my contemporaries. They grew up poor but determined. They formed the next generation after the first Great Migration.

Now in telling such stories, I am trying to give a picture of social change. Among my contemporaries, I am, I admit, a little bit of an exception, having married three times. In my younger days, divorce was looked down upon. Most of my peers settled down and stayed married. The children in my generation, whose grandparents had been slaves, grew up in fairly stable, two-parent households. This is well documented now. From 1910 to about 1950, 80 to 85 percent of black kids were in two-parent households. Now it's less than 35 percent. We see the same trends today in the white communities but not to quite as dramatic a degree. So society has changed, movements have changed. The way we live today is far different. I look back and am struck by the way black life has been altered, by the way we are now perceived in America. Our families of old were torn apart by the slave system, which sold babies away from mothers, and ripped husbands and wives from one another. What are the forces that tear children from parents and take loved ones from one another now?

I am so proud of and moved by the work and activism of young scholars who have documented the causes of these changes. But my intent here is not to write an academic book, only a collection of my memories. However, I certainly commend to you those who have written about such phenomena as mass incarceration, the decimation of public education, and the perpetuation of poverty among black Americans. I am moved by the work of those who have benefited from the advances of the civil rights movement, who are now teaching in our universities and on many other fronts. I am proud of them, but I'm not naming names here for fear of omitting some of these powerful intellects, many of them the children and grandchildren of the civil rights movement.

My intent in writing this book is simply to tell my story with as much humor, readability, and identification as possible, as well as some scholarship for those who want to check it out. I hope you'll enjoy it, and, typical as it may be, perhaps even be a little inspired by it to help make this world a better place. I hope, too, that you'll come to understand why I feel so much love for my Sacred Ground.

CHAPTER 1

You Come from People

"You come from people." That is what Mama would remind me. People who had been through slavery.

We had a history, as a people and as a family, and the ancestors were always a presence in our lives, in our home. Often when Mama or Daddy got upset or depressed, they would go off, sometimes to another room, to talk aloud to the ancestors. I grew up hearing them talking to the elders, often enough the elders who were no longer among the living.

But I never knew much about my family history before my grandfather on my daddy's side. They—his family—were split into two divisions. You took the slave master's name, and so we were both Blacks and Forneys. They were situated in Jacksonville, Alabama, and I guess the plantation must have been near there. My father did sharecropping near there, and they'd come pick him up to work their fields. These were people who I remember. I still have contact with their children, who still live in Birmingham. They didn't leave. I assume they were pretty well-off and chose to stay down south. Maybe they didn't want to deal with cold weather. Maybe they feared the breakdown of relationships in the North.

My daddy knew his father was from West Africa (Senegal, I later found out) and had arrived in this country through somewhere in North Carolina. After Emancipation, the slaves began to look for their family members and found many of them. My grandfather was a proud, tough man. After Emancipation, he was a farmer, and he had his own land. My daddy told me that Grandfather was walking down the street in Jacksonville, Alabama, with a cigar in his mouth, when he suddenly dropped dead in the street. He wore a suit and spats to go into town.

Now, William Lafayette Black, who owned the Black plantation, had been the *owner* of both my paternal grandfather and my paternal grandmother. His son, Hugo Black, who went on to become a U.S. senator and a justice of the Supreme Court, became a friend and a protector to my father. Hugo and Daddy grew up near each other on the plantation and remained in touch throughout their lives. These are facts. I'm not proud of it, but I can't throw these facts away. It was known around the Black plantation and in the area that my daddy was under Hugo Black's protection. My daddy could go vote, because he was under Hugo Black's protection. Hugo Black had been a member of the Klan when he was young, and when he joined the Supreme Court in 1937, I said to my daddy, "Did you hear they just put an ex-Klansman, Hugo Black, on the Supreme Court?" My daddy took a puff on his cigar and replied, "He'll be all right." I thought my daddy had lost his mind. He was a Garveyite, a follower of black nationalist Marcus Garvey, and he would not even allow a white person to come through our front door, and here he was saying that someone from the Klan would be all right. But Hugo Black went on to become one of the most progressive members of the court; he delivered the majority decision in the *Hansberry v. Lee* case, which challenged restrictive covenants, the agreements home owners and real estate companies used to enforce segregation in housing.

So the slave system not only made you take the name of the family who was using you to do the work, it could also create such conflicted feelings of loyalty. The American conundrum, I call it. But my grandparents were married, and this was a point of pride among us. The slave system could not break this family unit that they forged.

On Mama's side, McConner was their name—she became Mattie McConner Black—and the name was presumed to mean there were Scottish or Irish slave owners in their history. It was also inferred that we had some Scottish blood in our veins, courtesy of some master a few generations back, and perhaps from the Black side, my daddy's side, too. Mama also had some Native American ancestors.

My older sister, Charlotte, was not my blood sister. My father had been married before, to another woman in Birmingham. This first wife came into the marriage pregnant and then had my sister. She then betrayed my father and abandoned the family. This was before my father and mother met. So my father was raising this little baby girl on his own. When he married Mama, she raised Charlotte exactly as her own flesh-and-blood daughter. One day, when Charlotte was a teenager, she got into trouble. She stayed out all night. My mother met her at the door and said, "We've been up all night worrying about you." Charlotte yelled at Mama, "You're not my mother!" Suddenly, my daddy slapped Charlotte. Hard. At the time I had no idea what it was all about. He yelled at her, "She's all the mother you've ever had!"

Daddy's family ties in Alabama continued after we moved north. He kept in touch with the Caldwells and the Forneys in Birmingham, to whom he was fondly known as Uncle Dixie. My uncles Tom and Willie would come up to visit and bring their kids, who were a little younger than me. They would visit, but they would not stay for long. Conversely, we rarely went down south, other than for family funerals. My father was no longer comfortable there.

In 1918, before he moved his young family to Chicago, my father explored New York, but he found it too expensive and difficult to navigate. It was too sophisticated for him, and I think he knew it. I think Chicago was more comfortable for him. Perhaps he was attracted to the ample green spaces, wide midways, and expansive parks of Chicago's South Side. In those days, sheep actually grazed on the meadow at Washington Park. You could squint and pretend for a moment that you were back in the Alabama countryside. With in-laws and other relatives already having established households in Woodlawn, the South Side became the natural choice.

Anyway, my family, like so many, heard Robert Abbott's call to "Come North, young men." Again, Abbott was the publisher of the famous black newspaper the *Chicago Defender*, and he sent that paper, and that message, all over the South through the Pullman porters. My father and mother had migrated twice already: first from tenant farms where they chopped cotton to the market town of Florence, Alabama, and then on from there to the city of Birmingham. But the lure of a real, modern, northern metropolis was powerful. My daddy worked for Bessemer Steel in Birmingham, Alabama, and he could go work in the steel mills in Chicago, which he did, at U.S. Steel, before working in the stockyards. But like thousands of others leaving the South, Daddy was seeking not only economic opportunity; he also sought to remove his family from harm's way, from Klan terror. He was accustomed to carrying a pistol at all times, but he didn't want his children to grow up in that atmosphere. And my mama prized learning and culture above all; she wanted the best of schooling for her family. Those were the main reasons why blacks came up to Chicago—to be able fight back against white attackers, to get better jobs and be able to vote, and to get a better education for their children. Of course, the white businesses in the North wanted the blacks from the South for other reasons—to replace white workers going to fight in the war or going on strike.

My mama's mother had already settled in Chicago, along with an older sister. Between them, Chicago was the obvious choice. My aunt Lucille and uncle Henry had moved there first. But Henry proved to be an abusive husband. So Lucille, in need of an ally, brought her mother up to Chicago in 1915 or 1916, to assist and perhaps to mediate the domestic conflict, which ultimately ended in divorce.

Then there was Uncle Billy, one of my mama's brothers, who had left his Alabama home at the age of sixteen, hitchhiking north to Chicago. There he found a bar that offered cutting-edge jazz. Seated there as a newcomer to town, he found himself elbow-to-elbow with a familiar-looking gentleman. It was none other than his own older brother, Uncle Walter. They had not set eyes upon each other in years, since Billy was a youngster when Uncle Walter took off. Their almost genetic attraction to jazz had brought them to the same spot at the same moment in time, and once their eyes met, they took some moments to recognize them-selves as brothers.

Uncle Billy loved that neighborhood so much he settled into a Black Belt apartment at Thirty-First and State, in the center of the jazz district and at the height of the Jazz Age. Uncle Billy was drawn to the music, the energetic nightlife, and the ambience of relative freedom and cre-ativity that flowed through that neighborhood. (It is little known today, when a different part of Bronzeville, a couple of miles farther south, is marketed as the jazz district. But the real hub of jazz was just south of the Loop.)

With no formal training as a chef, Uncle Billy managed to snare a job on the railroad, rising from a cleaner to a cook. He became a well-known chef, and the big shots on the railroads would request Billy Thomas to cook for them. Thomas was of course the name of his parents' owners.

Uncle Billy prepared feasts for our whole family every time he was home on leave. He married a white girl who was university educated and the daughter of an Episcopalian bishop. Aunt Bertha fit right in to the family—she loved people, music, and ideas.

Uncle Billy opened one of the first outstanding BBQ stands in the city. People used to come from all over to Thomas's Barbecue on the fiftieth block of Grand Boulevard. Thomas's was the predecessor of modern chain restaurants. He invested in modern equipment, rotisseries and the like. Billy was a great success. He and Bertha had one child, my cousin Alice, and they all ended up living in the Douglas–Grand Boulevard area. I happily recall that on Sundays he'd take us riding in his car.

Uncle Walter McConner, another of my mama's brothers, and Daddy both resorted to strikebreaking when, in desperation, they were forced to take jobs in the steel mills while the all-white labor force was out on strike. Unfortunately, black strikebreakers were easily spotted. One night, Uncle Walter was riding home from that job on the streetcar when he was attacked by a group of whites who were looking for some blacks on whom to vent their rage. Walter fought them off, and managed to shove one with such force that the attacker fell out of the streetcar, striking his head on the pavement. Uncle Walter was charged with his murder. He was defended by the brilliant black lawyer Ferdinand Lee Barnett. Mr. Barnett was, incidentally, the husband of the journalist Ida B. Wells-Barnett, who campaigned against lynchings. Uncle Walter's case went all the way to the Illinois Supreme Court, where he was eventually acquitted of murder. But once the trial ended, he had to leave Chicago, for he was by then a marked man. Moving to Detroit, he worked in the Ford plant, became a union organizer, and was among the first in our family to own a car. His son, my cousin Walter Junior, was a nationally known track star from Cass Tech, the premier black high school in Detroit. Walter and his brother became entertainers during World War II. They were part of a special unit which provided diversion for the troops through athletic and acrobatic feats. And Walter went on to become a famous social worker; he devoted his life to helping troubled young people and eventually became the head of Children and Family Services in Chicago.

It may have been the labor issues, or the economy, or the racism that my daddy had to confront when going to work at U.S. Steel that eventually took him from the steel mills to the stockyards. I was never sure. He would leave home every morning dressed up in a suit and tie, whether he was going to the steel mills or the stockyards, and then change clothes at work. This was a way—not always effective—to avoid being harassed. He worked very hard to support us, whatever it took. I think I realized this at an early age. I remember one time, when I was six or seven years old, some of my friends were out with their fathers, who were taking everyone to this place or that, and they said to me, "Where's your daddy?" They were insinuating that my daddy didn't do such things with me. I felt angry at first, but then I thought about how my daddy would always take us out, to Washington Park or other places, whenever he did not have to work. And I thought to myself, "There's nothin' wrong with my daddy; there's something wrong with God."

Anyway, my daddy made the money, but my mama controlled it—she was the treasurer, and you always gave the money to her. Mama always wanted us to have some nice clothes, and one time she had bought us some things and she said to Daddy, "Dixie, look what I bought the kids." Daddy said, "Mattie, we can't afford that," but Mama said, "This is for the children, you're supposed to go into debt to get whatever they need." Daddy kept it up until finally Mama called him "an old shit ass." That was the only time I ever remember her swearing. Mostly they got along and sacrificed for their children. Mama would say do this, and Daddy would say, "Do what your mama says."

Black Metropolis

When we first moved to Chicago, we moved to the 4900 block of St. Lawrence Avenue. As was typical for those of us coming up from the South, we would move a lot—to 5012 South Calumet, to Forty-Ninth and Vincennes, and when I was in high school, to 5121 South Michigan. Also 5635 Calumet, 5000 Grand Boulevard, and finally 6230 Vernon, where my parents lived until my mama died. I had gone to four different schools by the time I was in second grade. But this was all in the same close community—Bronzeville, the Black Belt.

When we first got there, the area was predominantly white—mostly Bohemian, Estonian, and other white ethnics—but those whites soon ran away. My mother signed my siblings up for what was reputed to be the finest grammar school in the neighborhood. Typically she chose the school based on where the Jewish families sent their kids. As each barrier fell, my aunts would come over and say, "Have you heard? They are renting to colored over on —— Street," and Mama would pack up our household, and we'd move closer to what was believed to be the better school. This was the pattern for lots of families, and from then on it became an expanding black community. The powerful network of mothers moved us along.

In Chicago, people of color were often denied entry to restaurants or stores and could make scarcely any purchases outside of the Black Belt, so people like my relatives began to understand the necessity and the opportunity to develop their own business ventures. We were the original captive-audience marketing opportunity. When the first wave of the Great Migration began—even when it was just a trickle of folks coming from the South to Chicago—those first migrants generally came from mixed relationships. They were racially and socioeconomically mixed, and in most of the households at least one of the adults had gone to school, even to university, to a historically black college. Quite a few of those early, educated migrants passed for white. Their light skin and white features came from the harsh facts of slave history.

Now, even back in the nineteenth century, there were people like John Jones, who in 1871 became the first African American to hold elected office in Illinois. He was a prosperous tailor who owned a lot of land in the southern part of downtown Chicago. He was self-educated and an abolitionist who fought for black voting rights in Illinois, opposing the Black Code that denied blacks in Illinois their rights for much of the nineteenth century. He was an example to those who arrived later, with the first Great Migration. When they had experienced enough rejection and exclusion, they organized their own businesses. We always learned from the elders. You could not get a taxi to pick you up, so Jackie Reynolds and Mr. Bertel Daigre organized taxi and jitney companies. You had to wait to die until you could find a graveyard in which to be buried, so finally some people put together the money to purchase land and establish Burr Oak, the first black cemetery in Chicago and one of the first in the country. (My grandma and others of her generation could only be buried in a segregated section of the old Lincoln Cemetery.) T. K. Gibson, Frank Gillespie, and others brought into being Supreme Liberty Life Insurance Company, founded in 1919, because before them there was no insurance for people of color. Jesse Binga, who had built the first black-owned bank in Chicago, bought up the land at Thirty-Fifth and State Street, where today the Illinois Institute of Technology stands. Above the Binga Bank he installed a dance hall upstairs where we could go to dance parties.

One of the first black millionaires in Chicago was Anthony Overton. He was a trained chemist, and he felt that black women did not know how to get their skin changed [i.e., lightened] and still look like black women. He created Overton Hygienic Manufacturing Company and put a fleet of salesmen on the streets of the Black Belt. He had ladies like my mother selling his products out of their apartments. Neighbors would come over to buy from her. He also started the *Chicago Bee*, another influential black newspaper like the *Defender* and the *Whip*. People would say that the *Bee* would sting you, the *Whip* would whip you, and the *Defender* would defend you. The old Overton and Bee buildings still exist, on State Street, and are among the best of the Bronzeville landmarks. His daughter Eva Overton went to the University of Chicago and married Julian Herman Lewis, the first black to join the faculty there.

The Jones brothers were astonishing entrepreneurs. There were two sets of brothers, "GiveaDamn" and Teenan, and then Eddie, George, and McKissack. That second set contributed a lot to the economic life of Bronzeville, especially during the Depression. They supported relief efforts and even opened a Ben Franklin store on Forty-Seventh Street in 1937, the first black-owned department store. But their diverse businesses were based on capital derived from the policy (or numbers, and later lottery) business. Their father was a prominent minister in Vicksburg, Mississippi, but the family moved to Evanston, where the father became the pastor at Mt. Zion Baptist Church. His sons took a different road: the oldest, Ed, who became the king of the policy kings, dropped out of Howard University to make money as a Pullman porter before he found out he could make more money in policy. The brothers later moved to the South Side; their commercial interests were grounded there. They were policy men first and foremost. They turned gambling into a business that was identifiably black-owned. You could become an agent and work door to door or from your own house or from the back of a store. My mama even made a little money as an agent for them, collecting people's bets at our home. They gave lots of individuals a start in business. They controlled the business. There were others, but the Jones brothers were the most successful and independent; they did not work for the white gangsters. Many of the most successful institutions in my

Sacred Ground owed something to the Jones brothers, though the IRS eventually caught up with them.

By contrast, Ily and George Kelly, the Kelly brothers, had worked for the white mobsters. And for the Everleigh Club. Ily Kelly was a light-skinned guy, and he would take customers—famous political figures and prominent businessmen—to the famous Everleigh sisters' brothel, though he would drop his head and pretend not to notice who they were or what was going on. The Kelly brothers were educated but also into gambling. They learned the trade from working in Hyde Park early on as cleaners and waiters in the gambling joints. Like the Jones brothers, they were in a lot of conflict with the Chicago Outfit, which wanted to take over such a lucrative business.

There are many more I could name—Louis B. Anderson in the insurance business, Jim Knight, the first "mayor" of Bronzeville and a businessman and politician (also a policy king and the founder of the Palm Tavern, which was a front), and so on. When Oscar De Priest was asked by Mayor Bill Thompson to run for alderman in the old Second Ward, Jim Knight was a ward committeeman; Jim could and did tell the Republican mayor how to get the "Negro" vote, a role that would later be played, for the Democrats, by William Dawson under Mayor Richard J. Daley. Most blacks still voted Republican, so they needed a new strategy to mobilize and hold on to the political power of this voting bloc. And there were the Jacksons and the Rayners, who went into the embalming business. Sammy Rayner Junior went to Tilden High School with my brother, but left Tilden in order to attend a famous embalming school in Texas. Because the Rayners were Catholic they were allowed to conduct burials in Catholic cemeteries, but only in the segregated sections. It is a little-known fact, but there were quite a few black Catholics during this time.

So within the Black Belt we created these parallel economic institutions—essentially we built a parallel economy. And parallel cultural institutions and parallel social institutions—clubs, churches, fraternal and charitable organizations, sports and recreation leagues. We could work outside but would spend inside. And because of those parallel institutions, we could often work inside and spend inside. They used to say a dollar turned around at least five times within the Black Belt. "Don't spend your money where you can't work"—that was our slogan. That was the message sent out by Balm L. Leavell Jr. and Joseph

H. Jefferson, who launched another great black newspaper, the *Chicago Crusader* (originally the *New Crusader*) and founded the pioneering Negro Labor Relations League (NLRL) in 1937. As a young person, I owed a lot to Joe, especially, who was also on the board of the Wabash YMCA (where he tried, unsuccessfully, to teach me to swim).

Whites who had businesses inside the black community had to hire us in the black community. Today there are black folks who won't shop in an Arab-owned store or a Korean-owned mom-and-pop store in our neighborhood. They get angry about other folk who don't live here and who do nothing for the black community but take the money out, reinvesting not one penny in improving the neighborhood. There is a good deal of resentment. Many feel, well, Walgreens may be owned by whites, but at least Walgreens hires blacks. Those mom-and-pop stores will hire a young black man only to sit by the door as a security guard, but just like in the old days, they won't let a black employee punch the register.

Such was the neighborhood in which I grew up, with a sprawling, extended family of aunties, uncles, and watchful neighbors, as well as captains of industry, doctors, and artists. If you were black, this was where you lived, rich or poor. As the black population rapidly grew, it was densely packed within those boundaries, such that the average population in the Black Belt was 84,000 persons per square mile, compared to 21,000 whites per square mile just a few blocks outside the boundary. The boundaries were enforced by racism—physical violence, including bombings, as well as the enforcement of the restrictive housing covenants, the contractual agreements among property owners prohibiting the purchase, lease, or occupation of their premises by blacks or other people of color. Whole families occupied tiny apartments known as "kitchenettes," in which a large house would first be cut up into apartments, and then the apartments subdivided into mini-apartments consisting of one or two small rooms with a stove for both heat and cooking amid the living/sleeping space. But this was our Sacred Ground.

Belonging

The black families of that period, having left the South, tended to be relatively small. Seldom did a family have more than three children, mainly because of the limitations of space for them to live and the cost of raising a child.

Shortly after I was born, my mother had one more baby, a little girl, when we first got to Chicago. But my infant sister died of influenza in the 1918 epidemic known as the Spanish flu. My mother never got over that; she was left with a deep sense of guilt about losing her baby. I don't really remember the baby, having been just a toddler myself at that time, but she had a big impact on my early life. The loss of that baby meant that Mama took extreme care with me. I was always bundled up and overprotected. I could never wander far out of sight, maybe down to the corner. The neighbors all knew which child belonged to which household. I was known as Mattie's baby.

Although we moved frequently, there was always a neighborhood identity and a feeling of neighborliness. Both before and during the Great Depression, one did not feel a sense of shame or embarrassment about borrowing a necessity from the neighbors. We all did it. Nor was there a psychological feeling of depression. It was the Depression but we were not depressed. There was poverty, but we were not poverty stricken. We took care of each other. There was never a feeling of hunger or of not being able to get help to pay the bills or the rent. We never imagined we were going to starve or become homeless. Thus I do not recall being frightened.

For example, after my brother, Walter, graduated from Tilden High, the word got around that he was going off to the University of Illinois at Urbana-Champaign. That became a neighborhood project. The neighbors would ask, "What does Walter need?" They were so proud of their cousin or neighbor or nephew going to a predominantly white school. They would all chip in to make sure he would be successful, whether related by blood or not. That was pretty typical, especially for the young men and women going to mainly white schools.

When Walter went to the University of Illinois, there were about 11,000 students, of whom fewer than 100 were black. The majority of the black students were graduate students in the professional schools, but even there it was only a sprinkling. Here Walter met the woman who would become his first wife. Most of these graduate students had attended historically black colleges in the South for their undergraduate degrees, but when they sought to go to law school or medical school, they could not go to the graduate schools in the southern states, at places like Alabama or Oklahoma. So the state picked up the tab for them to come to Illinois or to the University of Chicago to get their graduate degrees. Even this accommodation was made for only a few students.

It was not until after the end of World War II that some relevant suits went forward, ending with the famous 1950 Supreme Court cases *Sweatt v. Painter* and *McLaurin v. Oklahoma*. In the second one, a plaintiff from Oklahoma, George McLaurin, had sought admission to the graduate programs of the state university. The District Court for the Western District of Oklahoma had ruled that McLaurin was eligible to go to the University of Oklahoma, and so he was admitted, but the university put him in separate living quarters. He could not stay in the regular university housing. This man had already graduated from the University of Illinois. In fact, he had many degrees and was a retired professor who wanted a doctorate in education. Thurgood Marshall, then chief counsel of the NAACP Legal Defense Fund, took up an appeal with the U.S. Supreme Court, and the Supreme Court's decision removed the restrictions. In *Sweatt v. Painter*, Heman Marion Sweatt, the civil rights activist who went forward as plaintiff, just wanted to go to law school in his home state of Texas, at the University of Texas. And ultimately, he won too, with the brilliant legal work of Marshall.

Anyway, Chicago's black neighborhoods all shared this pride of education. In that respect they were much like the Jewish neighborhoods. Again, among the blacks who came up from the urban South, many had at least some higher education. But in Chicago, my aunt Georgia was a servant even though she had gone to college. In the wealthy homes in Hyde Park and Kenwood, they wouldn't hire an uneducated servant. Georgia had been to college, but this was the best job she could get. Another of my father's brothers married an educated woman. They lived in Louisiana, and they offered to take Walter and educate him down there. But my dad wouldn't send Walter to live with them. We had left the South. We weren't moving backward.

So, when my brother got down to the University of Illinois, he could not live in a dorm or a frat house. He and most other black students boarded in the homes of local black families in Champaign. The university also had a couple of black fraternities and sororities, so there was an organized social scene. Walter and other black students worked as waiters and as cleaners in the white residence halls and fraternity houses. The coach would not even let him play on the basketball team, despite the urging of people like Lou Boudreau, who soon became a famous baseball player but at that time was captain of the basketball and baseball teams at the University of Illinois and an All-American basketball player.

When I was in high school, my basketball team from DuSable made it to the state championship high school tournament, the "Sweet Sixteen." And it was held at the big university gym in Champaign, of all places. But we were a sleeper. We were never expected to get that far. We took the state tournament by surprise. They had never had a black team come to the tournament, and no provisions had been made for people of color to have a place to stay. We had no place to practice. And yet, when the games took place, the stands were filled with people shouting for us to "play like the Globetrotters!" The Globetrotters were originally from Chicago's South Side; they started out in the 1920s as the Savoy Big Five, playing at the Savoy Ballroom. Anyway, the whole black population of Champaign came out to see us play. We lost, but among blacks we were heroes. That sense of community, of mutual support, was so important.

My Early Education

Mama and Grandma were my first teachers. Grandma, born a slave, had come up to Chicago from Alabama ahead of us. She was living with my mother's youngest sister, who needed her mother's help in her household. Having her mother and sister here was the main reason my mama wanted to move to Chicago.

Grandma loved me, and she pitied me because I was the "baby" after my younger sister died. So I was totally overprotected and closely supervised. Any mischief I committed I had to commit in the house. Grandma would ask me, "Baby, what's that you doin'?" I would of course assure her that I wouldn't do anything wrong (even when I was playing with matches). Her response was always the same: "*Baby, I cain't hear whatcha sayin' because whatcha doin' talks so loud.*" That was such a huge influence. It applies in political life, and still today, Grandma's voice echoes in my head. Sometimes she would say, "*What was ain't no is no mo,*" and we would all listen carefully to her—something important would follow.

I started kindergarten at Fuller Elementary. We had a beautiful teacher who treated us as if we were all her children. She was white. This helped me quite a bit psychologically to accept the notion that there were some very nice white people in my world. But I had one great calamity in kindergarten, which for a time made me a bit wary of leaving the house. One morning, as I was getting ready to go to school, my beloved grandma, who took such special care of me, said softly, "Oh, baby, Grandma doesn't feel too good today." After my half day at kindergarten, I came home for lunch, and Grandma was gone. She had died in the house that morning. That was the greatest sadness in my early life.

After kindergarten, I attended Forrestville and Frances Willard schools before I was sent to Edmund Burke Elementary School. I was an enthusiastic little school child. I loved books, I loved the little chairs, I loved to clap the erasers together for the teacher. I mean I really liked school. In our house, it went without saying that you would behave yourself in school.

One of my earliest school memories is a real heartbreaker. I met my first love in the second grade. She was tiny, dark-haired, and white. She was one of the Jewish children who attended Edmund Burke Elementary. I don't even know if I realized she was white. I can remember her face, but I can't remember her name. I think it might have been Sharon. I was all of seven years old.

In my class that year, we had to double up and share our readers. The school was becoming crowded, and there weren't enough books to go around. So when it came to reading time, all the kids paired up and shared. The lesson was all about "sharing with others." We were reading stories about children sharing playthings. This little girl and I pulled our two chairs next to each other and read from one book.

After a few minutes, I felt a hand gripping my shoulder. "Timuel," the teacher said in an icy tone, "return to your desk." So much for sharing. The teacher loudly admonished my little friend. "You. Go sit over there," she directed her, to sit next to and share the book with a white girl. Not with me. I couldn't look up. I felt cheated. Until that day, I had never been disciplined or even scolded in school. I knew that to get in trouble at school would bring hellfire at home, so I always behaved. Nor was I yet rebellious . . . that trait didn't kick in for a few more years. Yet suddenly, I seemed to be in trouble. But . . . for what?

When I got home that day, I did not tell Mama what had happened. I must have been confused, for I knew I had done nothing wrong. And yet . . . I obviously had done *something* to provoke the teacher's anger. Instead, I was angry with Mama. Why did she send me to a school where the teacher was so mean to me?

Flash forward at least fifteen years, to about 1940. I was a grown young man, of drinking age. In the waning days of the Great Depression, I frequented the clubs of Bronzeville—the Rhumboogie, the Palm Tavern, the Regal, and another one of my favorites, the Club DeLisa, a huge nightclub with one thousand seats, at State Street and Garfield Boulevard. It was a hot spot owned by the Mafia, but it catered to blacks, and it offered hot jazz and blues, a well-stocked bar, an ample dance floor, and an aura of risk and glamour. Rumor had it there was also gambling in the basement. Some of the greatest musicians and their bands played the DeLisa—and its in-house band, with percussionist Red Saunders in the driver's seat, was world famous.

The DeLisa was jumping, and I suddenly found myself face to face with my second-grade sweetheart. I had never seen her again since I was in short pants, but here we were. She, too, was all grown up. She was one of the few white girls in the joint. We spotted each other immediately, and amazingly, we still recognized each other. We both remembered that long-ago day in the second grade when the teacher had separated us. But the teacher wasn't around now. One thing led to another, and soon we were seeing a lot of each other.

But we still had a problem: I couldn't take a white girl home to meet my parents; my father would not have allowed her in the house. And she certainly couldn't take me home to meet her family, who still lived around Fiftieth and Michigan, where they owned a drugstore. It was one thing to *live* near blacks, or to sell to blacks. But dating and all that it implied was another matter altogether. When the two of us strolled in the neighborhood, the guys on the corner assumed that I must be a pimp, and that she was one of my "girls." Such were the complications of race. The relationship eventually cooled off. To this day, I can recall her face, but not her name.

I realize this story is a bit of a digression—but imagine how close a neighborhood would be in which such coincidences could take place.

Another time, when I was about that same age or a little older, I wanted to go to the White City Amusement Park with a white, Italian friend of mine, Joe Domino, whose father was the janitor at 5012 Calumet, where my family was living. It was a big amusement park over at Sixty-Third and South Park (formerly Grand Boulevard). So I asked my mama, and she dressed me up in my nice clothes, like my daddy when he went off to work. She knew there might be a problem. And there was. When we got there, Joe could go in, but they stopped me at the door. They said I wasn't dressed up enough. But Joe was not dressed up at all, and he could go in. He did not go because we were friends, and he would not go there without me. I was young, but I was learning about racism firsthand. White City was later sued by CORE [Congress of Racial Equality], in the 1940s, when they were still discriminating in this way.

Despite these unfortunate incidents, for most of my childhood I truly loved my school years, especially at Edmund Burke Elementary. To this day I'm still friends with a couple of my schoolmates from way back then. I was good at school, and we were able to safely walk to and fro without fear. We had some extraordinarily kind and altruistic white teachers who were not abusive and who spoke respectfully to our parents. Those elementary school years were good years. We spent our days playing every game kids could play in the street. We had less to worry about, it seems to me, than children do today. The worst thing that could happen to you was if your parents found out you were misbehaving. I do not remember ever worrying about getting shot or beaten up as a child, or feeling that danger and violence might lurk within the parks or playgrounds of my early years. All in all, I had a pretty carefree existence.

By the 1930s, we were doing moderately well economically, but it was always precarious. Suddenly, when my dad lost his job at the stockyards— kerplunk. We didn't have an extra nickel. I recall an awareness on the part of some of my peers that those fathers who worked for the post office or for the railroad were higher class and more prosperous. My daddy was working in the stockyards by that time, and that was already pretty low as far as social status was concerned. But now things were worse. Somehow, we managed. My father did odd jobs and even worked for the WPA [Works Progress Administration], until he was able to go back to his regular job.

During the Depression, while I was still at Burke, I would go across South Park—today Martin Luther King Jr. Drive—to hear the Reds speaking at the Washington Park speaker's forum. There were sometimes thousands of people there, many of them living in the park because they had been evicted from their homes. And sometimes one of the speakers would say, "Mrs. X has been evicted from her home," and we would all say, "Let's go put her back in." We would go take her furniture off the street and put it right back in her home. This was part of my political education. The oratory was powerful, and people would mobilize right there in Washington Park. That park has a very long political history, going back even before the famous Bud Billiken parade, which started in

1929 and was based on a fictional "Bud Billiken" character that appeared in the youth section of the *Defender* earlier in the twenties. That parade, now one of the biggest in the country, has always been an expression of the pride we felt in our Sacred Ground.

In 1932, I graduated from Burke Elementary School with my friend Bill Green. His dad worked at the post office so they were considered well-off. They had a big house, four bedrooms. They even had enough room in their home for a Ping-Pong table. In my childish view, that was a mark of expansiveness compared to the cramped quarters of many families. We'd be playing over at the Greens' house, and at a certain point, his mother would call out, "William, it's time for you to study." That meant, "See you guys later," and study he did. They were a good influence. Bill Green went on to become the first black IRS agent in the entire country.

High School Years—Our School, DuSable

The population of the Black Belt continued its rapid growth. It was four times as dense as any white neighborhood.

We were cooped up, and not only in terms of available housing for black residents of the South Side. We were also narrowly confined in terms of where we could attend high school. There was one high school which was deliberately designed to contain the black students—Wendell Phillips on Thirty-Ninth Street. I wanted to go there, but my mother believed strongly that Englewood High School was educationally superior. There was a mix of kids there, and it was not as crowded.

So I started out at Englewood. But I did not do well. I skipped a lot of school; I missed my friends who were at Phillips. I found many classes at Englewood dull. I could do in three days the work that was supposed to take four days. I did well in Latin and in algebra.

The white students at Englewood were the children of recent immigrants for the most part, except for the kids of Jewish merchants, some of whom lived in our neighborhood, over their parents' business establishments. There were some areas around the school where black students were not safe. Around Sixty-First and Wentworth the white kids were confrontational and would try to beat us up and chase us out of the neighborhood. At Englewood, we had some teachers who were quite good. But there was a lot of disparagement of the black students.

Teachers would ask the black students, in front of everyone, where their fathers worked. The fathers were at the post office or were Pullman porters. When I replied that my daddy worked at the stockyards, my classmates would hold their noses and laugh. The teachers would never ask those questions of the white kids. After a while, I went to class as little as possible.

Englewood's assistant principal was a notorious bigot. One day my friend Virgil and I were walking down the hall, and the AP stopped us and demanded to know who we were. I gave my real name, perhaps in an insolent tone of voice. My father was called. He came to the school. This administrator began to lecture my daddy—that was a mistake. My daddy responded in no uncertain terms: "I pay your salary and you don't pay mine. You don't tell me how to raise my children."

Still, I knew it was time to leave Englewood. I managed to flunk every subject but gym. Ultimately, I forged my mother's signature on transfer papers and transferred myself to Wendell Phillips, where I felt much more at home. Mama was upset when she found out, because in that part of the black community, Phillips was not prestigious. The rising high schools at the time were Lindblom, Tilden, Englewood, and Hyde Park.

At Phillips, where my older sister had gone, I found my elementary school pal Bill Green. His family had a lovely house at Thirty-First and Giles, so they wanted Bill to go to school in the neighborhood close by. Bill was glad to see me too. I didn't even know where the school office was. He showed me around, and they assigned me a homeroom. The first guy I met was Nat Cole, who became famous as Nat King Cole, the brilliant jazz vocalist and pianist; he sat right behind me in alphabetical order. We remained friends until he died many years later. But when we first met I did not even know he could sing.

Phillips was bursting at the seams with successive cohorts of new arrivals from the South. Finally, the school board agreed to build a second high school for the black community. Let me not give you the impression that this was out of concern for the well-being of the students. Quite the opposite. As blacks moved farther south, the school board did not want black students going to the predominantly white schools. I would say the decision to build a new high school—even in the midst of the Depression—was mostly a decision to expand the physical capacity of the school system to keep all or most of the black students in their place, so that we would not spread out across the whole city.

So they began building DuSable High School in the early 1930s to contain the growing black population. In February of 1935, a fire at Wendell Phillips sped up the process. We were moved over to DuSable before the building was even completed. I know that so well because we were supposed to have a basketball game that day. The fire affected the gym and auditorium. Very quickly they moved all of the Phillips faculty, staff, and students over to the new building. The carpenters and brick-layers were still working when we were crammed into the new space, which was initially titled New Wendell Phillips High School.

However, there was a group of active and educated women, mostly mothers, who met regularly at the George Cleveland Hall Library. Mama was among them. They were organized by Charlemae Hill Rollins, the children's librarian there, and by Vivian Harsh, the first black librarian in the entire Chicago Public Library system. Miss Harsh herself had graduated from Phillips, which had been built around 1903. These women would get together regularly. Among them were some wives of black men who were doing well in politics. They wanted the new high school to be truly excellent, and they demanded that the new building be named after Jean Baptiste Point du Sable, the first non-native settler on the banks of the Chicago River. The original name was "De Saible" but that lent itself to some racist jokes about "disabled," so the name became "DuSable." DuSable was black, a Haitian, and he married a Native American woman.

At that time the northern boundary for DuSable was Forty-Third Street, with Cottage Grove and the Rock Island Railroad tracks forming the eastern and western attendance boundaries, and Sixty-Third Street on the south. Phillips had its boundary from Forty-Third up to Twenty-Fourth and the same east and west borders. If you look at a map of Chicago, even today, you can see that this was really nothing more than a strategy of containment. The same strategy applied some twenty years later, when the school board began adding "temporary" portable classrooms to the school playgrounds in the Black Belt to keep black children from transferring out of overcrowded elementary schools. These trailers, known as "Willis Wagons" after Superintendent Benjamin Willis, were a concrete manifestation of racial segregation. They were completely unsuitable as a learning environment for children, but that was not their real purpose.

With our booming population density and the competition for status and prestige, many black families lived much better on the West Side and in the area referred to as the Gap. As for my mother and her child-hood friends from Florence, Alabama, there was some competition for who had the most talented and academically successful children and who went to the best schools.

Florence, Alabama, remained a touchstone in our lives, even decades after the immigrants came to Chicago. When my late son—I will say more about him later on—was attending Stanford University, he observed: "Dad, you know, everybody I ever heard of that came out of Florence went to college." And it was true. There were teachers from Florence and the children of immigrants from Florence all throughout the school system.

I am not alone in my thinking of DuSable as the first school that was really ours. I felt at home there. I was able to excel and so were so many others. Even though I was never among the tall kids, I had a love for basketball and I was competitive. My brother, who was a lot taller than me, was the star player over at Tilden, which took the city championship in 1935. He could have played for the Globetrotters—Abe Saperstein wanted him to, but Mama said no, he was going to college (and the University of Illinois would not even let him play). But I tried out and made it onto the DuSable team, which, as I said, eventually made it to the state championship high school tournament, the "Sweet Sixteen." I learned so many valuable lessons playing basketball. Al "Runt" Pullins, who was one of the original Savoy Big Five and then a famous Harlem Globetrotter, was only a couple inches taller than I was, but he became a great player. One time he was watching a bunch of us young people play, and he called me over and told me, "Shorty, when everyone else is run-ning up and down the court acting crazy, you stay cool and you'll break up the game." That was good advice, and I've always tried to remember it. Stay cool.

But the most famous attribute of DuSable was its music. It had argu-ably the greatest high school music teacher ever, Captain Walter Dyett. Don't take my word for it—just look him up and see all the world-class musicians he personally trained. People would use fake addresses just to get to attend DuSable so they could study with Captain Dyett, whose "Hi-Jinks" musical performances featured high school musicians who played like professionals. So many of my classmates there went on to become famous, in all fields—John Johnson, the publisher of *Ebony* and *Jet* magazines; Nat King Cole; the judge William Cousins; the comedian

Redd Foxx; Dempsey Travis, who was in music and real estate and later became a historian; and Harold Washington, the first black mayor of Chicago, though he was a few years younger. Later graduates included Dinah Washington, the jazz singer, and Harlem Globetrotter Nat "Sweetwater" Clifton, who is in the Basketball Hall of Fame, and many more great musicians, artists, businessmen, athletes, and politicians.

I love getting together with all the DuSable alumni. We have a very active alumni association, with great friends like Alice Brown keeping us all in touch.

DuSable also had, for a school motto, some famous words from the abolitionist Wendell Phillips carved over the auditorium stage: PEACE IF POSSIBLE, BUT JUSTICE AT ANY RATE. These words have stayed with me, even though my father had a lot of doubts as to whether we could change the United States. If you couldn't change it, he argued, you ought to think about going back to Africa. Like so many in our community, Daddy had great respect for Marcus Garvey. But Mama insisted that no, we're going to integrate, we're going to fix the injustices, we're going to change it. What they agreed on was that change *had* to come, and that change was *going* to come, one way or the other.

Becoming an Organizer and a Salesman

When the Depression really hit full blast, in the early thirties, my big brother Walter dropped out of high school for a time, over the vehement protests of my parents. He wanted to help the family. He went to work in a nearby grocery store. Walter stayed out of high school for two years, during which time my mother never ceased to demand that he go back to school. And eventually her campaign was victorious.

Walter returned to finish high school, having fallen a few semesters behind his contemporaries at Tilden High, but he caught up with them down at the University of Illinois. These were outstanding young men like Earl Strayhorn, who went on to become a distinguished judge in Chicago, and John Rogers [Sr.], who became a Cook County judge. Rogers later served as a member of the Tuskegee Airmen, and his son would become the founder of Ariel Investments and serve on the board of trustees at the University of Chicago. Walter went on to an extraordinary career as a civil rights lawyer and political strategist himself. After the war he graduated from John Marshall Law School and worked for several law firms, like McCoy, Ming, and Leighton, where he became a partner in 1952. Later he helped Richard Hatcher get elected mayor of Gary, Indiana. Hatcher was the first black mayor of Gary; Hatcher and Carl Stokes, of Cleveland, were the first black mayors of major cities in the U.S.

When Walter went back to high school, I inherited his job in the grocery store, though I stayed in school. After my lengthy "career" of selling newspapers on a street corner (mostly the *Defender*), this was my first actual job, in a mom-and-pop grocery where my big brother had worked, on Fifty-First Street between Indiana and Michigan Avenues. The owners were Jewish and lived in Hyde Park. The store was simply entitled Louis Kaplan's Store. There were very few chain stores in the area. I began as a porter, sweeping up, and as a delivery boy, employing my red wagon or my bicycle, depending on the size of the order.

I was about thirteen or fourteen years old and thrilled to have this job, so I was a conscientious and enthusiastic worker. I felt so grown up and just loved the idea that I was contributing to the family. But shortly after I started working in Louis Kaplan's Store, "St. Louis" Kelly arrived in town and shook up my outlook.

J. Levert Kelly, president of the Waiters and Bartenders Union, a man with connections to the Outfit, walked into the store and said to me, "Say, you're a bright fellow. Why aren't you punching the register?" He would walk in and—wham! He'd knock all the cans off the shelves, and he'd turn and tell the guy who swept the floor, "Hey you, go punch the register!"

Kelly was making several points: One, that we were smart enough to do it. Two, that there was power if we got organized. Three, that the white shop owners couldn't really survive without us. It was a combination of winning by intimidation and by shrewd organizing.

At that time we were making something like twelve bucks a week, working seven days a week. We often worked long hours, more than ten or twelve hours a day. Some of the owners lived upstairs from their stores. Some of them lived right in the neighborhood. They needed to maintain decent relations with their customers and with the workforce. And here we were, working dawn to night, all day Saturdays, and half a day on Sundays. After school, we'd work for a few hours and then go home and do our homework. All this for twelve bucks a week. That money was a genuine help to our families. There was no welfare, no health insurance, no Social Security. The New Deal was just getting started. So we were glad to have any job. The idea was that we would help the family. But we were kids. Kelly talked to us, and he gave us the bigger picture that we were too young and inexperienced to see at first.

At the time when St. Louis Kelly began to organize, we could not join the whites-only retail clerks union. But with our help, Kelly was able to form the Colored Retail Clerks Union. We covered every retail store, whether family-owned or corporate, such as the A&P and Consumers. We were hugely successful. And in less than a year, our salaries jumped from twelve to eighteen dollars a week, with a day off every week and one week's paid vacation every year. That was really a triumph.

Having a job in the neighborhood was a pleasure; you walked to work, you knew everyone, and you didn't have to face the daily racism, like my daddy faced at the steel mills and the stockyards. Plus, we were making a real contribution to the well-being of our families. Even when the Depression was at its worst, the sense of poverty never seemed that overwhelming. We always lived in and around fairly prosperous neighbors, among doctors, lawyers, railway porters, and postal workers.

The church was also a very important thing for us young people. They offered us social and athletic programs—we played basketball at the churches, and met girls. One of the first places my family visited in Chicago was Quinn Chapel A.M.E Church, the historic black church that had played such a big role in the Underground Railroad. At first we were members there. My mama had been a Presbyterian in Alabama, but when she married my daddy she joined the A.M.E. Church—the African Methodist Episcopal Church. My daddy even became a deacon in the A.M.E. church we later attended, which was the one over on Evans in Woodlawn. One time, one of my daddy's friends asked him if God knew about the situation of black folk, and Daddy cracked, "He knows. He just doesn't care." But then the next Sunday, like every other Sunday, we all went off to our church. We went to church every Sunday and there were many recreational activities for kids, which were basically free of charge.

In fact, we rarely left the neighborhood. All our entertainment was close by, including the Willard Theatre, the Metropolitan, and the Owl Theatre at Forth-Sixth and State Streets. The big one was the Regal, but I loved the Owl. Its pit band was very popular. So on the weekend, after we'd get off work, we'd go have fun. As I said, it was the Depression, but we were not depressed. We had the churches, the clubs, and some jobs.

Chicago had a couple of thriving and huge hotels, even during the Depression. The hotel workers and the waiters in the hotels were originally organized with the sleeping car porters. The hotel and restaurant workers were well-spoken and educated, yet they made more in tips than in wages. They were often quite sophisticated. Most of their children went on to college. They worked in an atmosphere that was cosmopolitan. There was the Stevens Hotel (later the Hilton), one of the biggest hotels in the entire country, built by the father of Supreme Court Justice John Paul Stevens. And there was the Palmer House, perhaps the most famous and elegant of the downtown hotels. Blacks couldn't stay in these hotels, but we worked in all of them. Potter Palmer, the owner of the Palmer House on State Street, had it written into his will that the jobs of waiters in his hotel would belong to Negroes in perpetuity. He meant this as a benevolent gesture, reserving for the benefit of the Negroes a set of subservient jobs in his hotel. It's that old American conundrum.

By the time I was fifteen or sixteen I had two part-time jobs. I was still working for Louis Kaplan, but I also worked on Forty-Seventh Street at a combination optical and jewelry store in the South Center Building, one of the larger commercial buildings in the area. The owners of the jewelry story were Polish Jews. They heard what was happening in Europe, and the wife went to visit her family back in Poland. She returned to Chicago in tears.

We were becoming aware of the gathering danger. Our teacher at DuSable, Miss Mary Herrick—and I will say more about her a little later—assigned us to listen to the radio, to pay attention to the speeches of Hitler. The saying went "Hitler wants peace on earth . . . a piece of Poland, a piece of Czechoslovakia . . ." and so on. I had a deep feeling of dread about what was happening in Europe in the early thirties. Most of my white friends were Jews. I had learned a little Yiddish. At the store, the owner used to speak to us in Yiddish. I learned how to sell. I learned about small business, even though I was still going to school and playing basketball. And I was learning about the political situation.

During the Depression there began to be greater cohesion between black and white radicals. Their activities in our neighborhood focused upon Washington Park. The radical organizers—communists, socialists of every description—held public forums and debates in the park at the famous Washington Park forum, as well as downtown in the park known as Bughouse Square. My friends and I would go listen to the speakers and organizers, and we'd debate their merits, the merits of brilliant speakers like Claude Lightfoot and Ishmael Flory. The communists had made a big impression by defending the Scottsboro Boys, the nine black teenagers falsely accused of raping two white women in Alabama in 1931; they defended them when many other civil rights organizations would not.

Anyway, in that context, St. Louis Kelly recruited me to be a union organizer. The Negro retail union had an office at Forty-Seventh and South Park. When we began to organize, the shop owners tried to fire us, but we closed down the stores. My mama and daddy were proud of me for doing it. When Mr. Louis Kaplan fired me, I got another job at another grocery. I don't know what it was about, but when St. Louis Kelly heard they had fired me, he told Mr. Kaplan: "You just fired him but I just hired him, and he'll be there." In that segregated enclave there was an understanding of power. I immediately landed another job because of the union, and after Kelly called him, Mr. Kaplan offered to rehire me. I could have gone right back to that same store but there would have been tension.

We were now coming up against the possibility of world war. I remember sitting in my pal Cleo "Tally Ho" Smith's house predicting that it would not be too long before the U.S. would be at war. We were kids, but we all talked about the social and cultural issues—even in the pool room, "Dad's Very Safe Pool Hall." We observed, and we talked about, the status of blacks and where the world was going.

And we had teachers who looked beyond the immediate, who were truly dedicated to their students. Miss Herrick knew every one of our names and kept track of where we were. She wrote to most of her former students when they were in the army. Miss Herrick was white, and she had attended the University of Chicago. She was a very big influence on my life, as I will explain in more detail later on.

Contributing to our dawning political interest was the fact that we also had a few black agitators among our teachers. That's where I first got exposed to black history. Mr. Dorsey, a history teacher, concentrated on black history. We didn't even know that Egypt was part of Africa. We thought it was Europe. Mr. Lucas told us in 1935 that sometime somebody was going to split the atom. The implications were not clear yet.

The groundwork had been laid at Phillips for us all to go to Xavier University in New Orleans. That was a basketball school. They even played the Globetrotters—this literally put Xavier on the map. I started out there but didn't stay long. We were about the third cohort of students to go down there. Lucius Thomas and Henry Blackburn were from Tilden, but the rest of us were from DuSable. I went to Xavier, but I was too distracted by the girls at Xavier.

I had graduated from DuSable in January of 1937. Our senior prom was held across the street at Bacon's Casino, the site of Joe Louis's first professional fight, and of the famous "breakfast dances" that my big brother Walter would go to, at six in the morning! But after high school I couldn't find a job that paid anything much. I had broken with the grocery store where I had spent much of my teen years. Walter, who had graduated from the University of Illinois in 1939, was now working in Milwaukee at the Greenbaum Tannery. He was brought up there to play on the company's basketball team. I went up there to join him, and they recruited me to the team too.

In Milwaukee, Walter and I lived in a rooming house. There was almost no talk about the war at that time. After the German-Soviet Pact in August of 1939, I talked to my left-wing friends, asking what they were going to do now. And later on, of course, after Germany invaded it in 1941, Russia came over to be an ally. But earlier on, before the U.S. entered the war, and because there were so many German people in Milwaukee, as well as a lot of Jews, there was almost no public talk about the war. It was almost rude to bring it up.

Now in Milwaukee, none of the beer companies hired any blacks. The Urban League was working to get a lot of young blacks hired, especially young men with families. We were part of the Fur and Leather Workers Union, and the secretary of this union was both a Jew and an open member of the Communist Party. He came into the Greenbaum Tannery to organize the union, and we helped. It was not our first time organizing a union.

Once the Greenbaums got wind of our union-organizing activities, they fired me, and I came back to Chicago. I started selling funeral policies and other insurance at about twenty-one. When I first got back from Milwaukee, I went to work at Jackson Insurance. But then someone told me I was not making enough money so I switched to the Metropolitan Funeral System, a burial society. They had bought a piece of land to put up a fancy headquarters. The wealthy Madam C. J. Walker's inspiration and rival, Annie Turbo Malone, sold them the land for the Metropolitan Insurance Building on Forty-Fifth and South Park. She had a beauty college there called Poro College that filled the entire block. They taught how to style the hair of black men and women. You could make a lot of money in that business. Annie Malone was quite a lady and a great philanthropist, as were Madam C. J. Walker and the woman who ran her Colleges of Beauty, Marjorie Stewart Joyner, who was based in Chicago and very politically active. They opened the doors for many young women and used their wealth to combat lynching and other injustices. When Sarah Breedlove (Madam Walker's real name) died in 1919, even W. E. B. Du Bois wrote an admiring obituary.

The Met built their new headquarters, and in back of it was a garage and a modest air strip where they began to train young men to fly. Flying became such a popular thing with blacks at that time; Bessie Coleman had led the way, in the twenties. Some of the teachers were local guys who had volunteered to go to Ethiopia, the only country in Africa that had not been a victim of colonialism, and a place we greatly admired in our community. They brought back the stories of the Italians and how they treated the Ethiopians. They were not afraid to die defending Ethiopia. And this all took place on Annie Malone's land. Her personal pilot was John C. Robinson, the father of the Tuskegee Airmen.

At the Met we had people who had been Pullman porters who went into the insurance business as well as the policy business. Most of the salesmen there were from places where they had been insurance agents, like Atlanta and Memphis. They were pros. They knew the business. When I came, we had an instructional course on selling insurance. Almost all of the sales force were college grads, and we really learned how to succeed in that business. I was making and spending all that money and not saving anything.

I came back to Chicago about the time of the Supreme Court's 1940 *Hansberry v. Lee* decision, which involved a suit by Carl Augustus Hansberry, the father of Lorraine Hansberry. He was a very successful businessman, a real estate broker, and one of those who turned the apartment buildings into kitchenettes, putting two or three units into what had been a regular apartment. But he hated segregation and moved his family into a white section of the Washington Park subdivision of Woodlawn (the Washington Park subdivision of Woodlawn is adjacent to, but not the same as the Washington Park neighborhood, and is the site of the old horse racing track just to the south of the actual park). The Woodlawn Property Owners' Association, with help from the University of Chicago, had helped promote the use of restrictive covenants in that area, and Anna M. Lee and other white property owners got the courts in Illinois to rule that the restrictive covenant in question was binding and enjoined the Hansberry family from occupying that property. But Mr. Hansberry appealed that decision, challenging restrictive covenants, and the case went to the Supreme Court. He was represented by the great Earl Dickerson. The Supreme Court rejected the particular restrictive covenant that had been used against him, but it did not settle the matter of restrictive covenants in general. Even so, it was the beginning of the end of restrictive covenants, and the Supreme Court's *Shelley v. Kramer* decision in 1948 would render them practically useless, unenforceable.

My family at this time moved to 6230 South Vernon in Woodlawn, just a few blocks away from Mr. Hansberry's property at 6140 South Rhodes, the place where Lorraine Hansberry lived when she was young and that inspired her play *A Raisin in the Sun*, with its accurate depictions of the racism of the day. Apparently, however, our new white neighbors were unaware of the Supreme Court ruling. We also soon learned how bigoted, prejudiced, and violent the people just north and northwest of Sixty-Third in the Woodlawn area were. When we moved in, the whites decided they were going to keep it for themselves. But they underestimated us. After a few skirmishes they quit.

Anyway, at the Metropolitan Funeral System, I was making one hundred bucks a week and having a good time. My debit—the list of my steady clients—was located between Pershing Road and Thirty-First on Oakwood Boulevard. This was becoming a lively nightlife area. There was a hotel at Oakwood and South Park that held the Grand Terrace—the regular venue of Earl "Fatha" Hines. White entertainers lived at this hotel, including Mrs. Marx, mother of the Marx Brothers.

I could go in the bar and meet people like Fats Waller, sign them up as customers for our funeral insurance policies, and they would pay me a full year's premium just because they liked me. Up and down that street, and on Forty-First Street and Thirty-Ninth Street, I built a successful network of clients. There I met the talented and later quite famous singer Sam Cooke, who used to sing outside the bar; he couldn't sing inside because he was too young. We used to give him money, never guessing how successful he would become, with great songs like "A Change Is Gonna Come."

Anyway, I had built the debit—my clientele—into a solid operation. A few years later, when I was in the army, people in that debit would still write to me.

By 1940, Congress could see the writing on the wall. They passed the Selective Service Act, and even though it was still peacetime, we were supposed to register for the draft. I registered for the draft at the Carter School, at 5728 South Michigan. All this time, Mama kept talking to me about "When are you going back to school?" She really wanted me to get myself to college. But I had money in my pocket, and I was in no hurry.

Then one day I got a letter from the draft board. My father was against the war. He wasn't antisemitic, but he didn't think blacks should participate in the military while we were not being treated equally at home. There were terrible race riots in New York City and in Detroit, where we had family. In Milwaukee they drafted all the unmarried young black men. For a time, I left town to avoid the draft. The male population was suddenly disappearing. The young girls were getting a bit desperate. So I had a good time, meeting all these famous people, enjoying myself.

On December 7, 1941, I went out to celebrate my twenty-third birthday along with Joe Bowles, who was a physician, and George Oliver, the playwright. We sat in the 411, owned by Ily Kelly, the numbers operator (the bar was a front, like the Palm Tavern and other bars). Somebody ran in and shouted, "Pearl Harbor has been bombed!" "Well," I wisecracked, "she shouldn't have drank so much." But one of the neighbors knew exactly where Pearl Harbor was, and she didn't find it funny. "You know they got my babies there," she said. Her children had gone to Hawaii for jobs at the end of the Depression. Our two cousins were there. Mama called the Red Cross, and they found that these two boys had not been hurt.

When I received the message of greetings, I tried to ignore it. I said, "I don't have an Uncle Sam." But I was finally inducted in August of 1943, two years after the attack upon Pearl Harbor.

The army gave me my first uncoached experience in the South. The forties, and not just Pearl Harbor but my induction and service, reinforced a feeling that I had had when I was younger. We used to talk in the pool room and in each other's homes about injustice, but when I saw the war and the injustices of places like Buchenwald, that was something else.

CHAPTER 2

All That Jazz

Before moving on to the World War II years, I would like to add this brief interlude about my lifelong love affair with jazz.

What is it about jazz that grabs me, calms my spirit, focuses my mind? I enjoy jazz almost every evening. It is my tranquilizer after the cares of the day. It provokes memory and imagination and relaxation. It shows that there is no monopoly on joy.

Our family listened to all kinds of music. But it was jazz that grabbed me, and it has held me all my life. At the age of three or four, I was already hooked. I first heard Louis Armstrong when I was at most five years old. I had friends, long before I ever met Nat Cole in high school, who were playing jazz as children. You couldn't walk down a street in this neighborhood, any street, and not hear some jazz. There were teachers all over, musicians who supplemented their income by giving lessons. I didn't learn how to play, but I was so crazy about jazz that when I heard Duke Ellington and then saw Johnny Hodges, I became captivated.

My daddy worked hard. When he got a job at the U.S. Steel mill in south Chicago, he worked a ten- or twelve-hour day. But on Saturday we would enjoy music together. On Sunday, we'd go to church and hear some good gospel or some spiritual music. We'd come home, and Daddy would put on Ethel Waters or Louis Armstrong, and we'd dance and share our feelings of spirit together. I know this is no longer the scheme of life. But this is what music can do. You want it to do what that music did for our families and for our sense of community—even across racial boundaries, as occurred when Tommy Dorsey and other whites began to come into our area to hear and share jazz.

As a kid, what I wanted was to play alto sax. What my mama wanted was for me to play piano. She gave me the money to go take piano lessons at Warwick Hall with Erskine Tate, a big-time bandleader who played in the pit bands of the movie theaters when films were silent. The multitalented Mr. Tate was a jazz violinist, a pianist, *and* a composer. His extraordinary band gave many top artists their start. In his big band, at various times, he had Louis Armstrong, Fats Waller, Teddy Wilson, and so many of the greats. He also gave music lessons, as did the members of his band. I'd usually walk right on past Mr. Tate's place and spend the money going to the movie theater instead. I did learn where middle C was, and I could play "Little Boy in a Boat." But when Mama found out what I was up to, she stopped giving me the money for lessons.

Years later, I returned to Warwick Hall as a teenager. The hall was the live performance venue in the Warwick Hotel at Forty-Seventh and St. Lawrence Avenue. Many big bands played the Warwick, and the bands of high school–aged musicians were wildly popular. Several professional musicians had studios in the building, including my momentary piano teacher Erskine Tate.

In the 1930s, Warwick Hall offered afternoon dance parties a few times a week, and "Battle of Rhythm" competitions, where teens could socialize and dance to live music. Many of the bands who performed there featured outstanding high school musicians like my DuSable classmate Nat Cole and his "Rogues of Rhythm," and the multitalented Ray Nance—singer, trumpeter, violinist—who attended Wendell Phillips High School and went on to play and collaborate with Duke Ellington. There was Tony Fambro, who went to Hyde Park High and played the alto sax. Fambro gave his band the daring name "Jungle Rhythm Orchestra." These were all youngsters from the neighborhood who went on to establish musical dynasties. The older musicians who played in the pit bands were their mentors and coaches. Earl "Fatha" Hines, arguably the greatest pianist of the day, loved to sit at the piano with Nat Cole and encourage him.

I am neither a musicologist nor an academic expert on music. But I guess when you live this long, you stumble across some information. My childhood and my adolescence happened to occur in the height of the Jazz Age, and nowhere was that period richer or more alive than in our South Side neighborhood, my Sacred Ground.

Again, we were very densely packed into our ghetto. When I say *ghetto*, I refer not simply to poverty, but to the confinement, as was true in the Jewish ghettos in Europe. You were confined because of race. All the social classes were here. And the parallel institutions that we created helped us to get and somehow control that which we needed to survive, including our culture, our arts. We had a movement of socially conscious artists in all fields—revolutionary visual artists like my friends Margaret Burroughs and Charles White, playwrights and novelists, dancers and poets, and above all, musicians. We had everyone from Archibald Motley to Richard Wright and Langston Hughes, but the musicians still stand out. Under these conditions arose our uniquely American classical music: jazz.

After human beings showed up on this earth more than a million years ago, there were three fundamental things they had to have in order to survive: food, clothing, and shelter. These are universals. Everyone needs them. But after you get these three, what do you do next? Now that you're feeling pretty comfortable, you want to have some fun. And the way to have that fun is to be creative. It can be art, it can be athletics. But for many, if not most people, it's music—either making it or enjoying it.

In the confines of ghettoization, you may possess the academic or mechanical qualifications to fit into the larger world, but you may not have the social or political opportunities. We had lots of musicians. Our early jazz musicians were, for the most part, classically trained. Yet they could not get employment as symphonic musicians. In the period just before and during World War I, our jazz musicians became extremely popular. Some of them went off to Europe during the war, never to return to America. Black musicians continued to live in France, Switzerland, and other countries, where they found that their music was accepted and enjoyed.

Many experts have observed that jazz is a combination of the African beat and the European melodic line. Now I don't know how accurate that definition is. But I do know that the combinations and endless variations of those diverse national and international themes and rhythms, and the act of sharing them, bring people together to appreciate the wisdom of their backgrounds.

So jazz was what joined us together—me and many others who didn't know how to play a single note (or at least not many). On the blocks where we lived, there were no nightclubs or jazz clubs. We had what they called a Grafonola in the house, and later, a Victrola. The Grafonola had a big morning-glory horn on it, and you had to crank it in order for it to play. We had in the house the classical music of Brahms and Mozart and all that stuff. My mama wanted to be sure we could go wherever life might take us and talk about Paderewski. That was part of our upbringing. But we also had some Bessie Smith and some Mamie Smith. And there was Louis Armstrong, whom I just adored.

When I was just five years old, Mama took my brother Walter and me to the Vendome Theater on Thirty-Third and State Street. And there I heard this magnificent sound. Louis Armstrong. I had never heard anything like that. It was for me as a small child a sound so profound and embracing. I was absolutely hypnotized by the music of Louis Armstrong. That was the day I fell in love with jazz.

There was only one problem. In mid-concert, I needed to go to the washroom. But, gripped as I was by the spell of the music, I forgot I had to go. Nature took its course . . . I was only a small boy. I pissed my pants, but I never regretted it, because I didn't want to miss a note of this new sound. From that point on, I became addicted to that sound and those beats. It was different. As a child I was immersed in it. I could not have explained or defined what it was that I loved, but the sound of Louis Armstrong's horn became my favorite sound. There were so many around us making music— Earl Hines, Jimmy Lunsford, and a great many whose names are not well known, like Eddie Johnson, an old classmate from Burke Elementary.

In the 1920s in the old neighborhood, quite a number of theaters opened, such as the Vendome. Chicago's black South Side had a strip of entertainment venues along State Street we called *The Stroll*, from Twenty-Sixth Street to Thirty-Ninth Street. This was before Forty-Seventh Street had the big theaters. You could walk the entire Stroll and not escape that beat and those melodic lines floating from the bars and nightclubs and theaters. Day or night. You'd feel better, because everybody's clapping and shaking their hips walking down the street. The ladies shook more than the men. This music inspired more freedom in them. We appreciated that.

In that entertainment district, we began to get a mix of musicians. It was quite a sensation when Benny Goodman came over from the West

Side to listen and learn. He brought with him other musicians, known as the Austin High School gang. They began to show up and sit in and play with the black musicians. When I was still a little guy we would watch these people of different complexions playing and practicing with one another. That was a new experience for a kid like me, whose family had fled the South when I was so young, to see this kind of relationship and the feeling of brotherhood based on the entertainment and creativity that they enjoyed together.

Benny Goodman later broke the race barrier by bringing Lionel Hampton and Teddy Wilson into his band. He was the first of the white bandleaders to break the color line. Lionel was from Chicago and went to St. Elizabeth's, a Catholic high school in our neighborhood. We all knew each other. The evolution of jazz was continuing, but now it was being shared. Benny Goodman became popular among black audiences.

Now, I have a particularly important memory of Benny Goodman, but I need to explain the context. In 1936, when I was close to graduating from high school, Joe Louis, the heavyweight fighter, was defeated by Max Schmeling. Joe was black, and Schmeling was not only German, but a Nazi symbol, a willing symbol of white supremacy. That was a sad day, but the music gave us some inspiration. The disappointment of that defeat was shared by our Jewish neighbors. There was an affection between us and the Jewish community that both surrounded and was a part of the Chicago Black Belt. Again, Jewish merchants lived among us, over their shops and on the edges of the neighborhood. We had a kinship that was hard to describe. Our generation was emerging from post-slavery in a fantastically racist period.

On the night of the big fight, everyone listened on the radios. Blacks were saddened at the outcome, and among our friends who were Jewish, I saw their mothers and fathers were crying. Their relatives in Europe were being terrorized and worse. And we didn't even know the full extent of it yet.

In 1936, at the Olympic Games in Berlin, Jews were not to be allowed to participate. But from our neighborhood, we had the great Jesse Owens and Ralph Metcalfe as part of the United States delegation. We all knew them; we were cheering them on, and we followed their every race and celebrated every victory. They swept the Olympics, infuriating Hitler. At home and in Europe, jazz—American jazz, Chicago jazz—got a huge lift from this victory.

But 1937 would give us another huge lift.

In 1937, when we learned that Benny Goodman had incorporated two black musicians in his band, we decided we had to go and see this. They were scheduled to play in the "Battle of the Bands" over at the Eighth Regimental Armory in the thirty-fifth block on Giles Avenue. This armory was built in 1915 and was the first built specifically for an all-black military regiment, the "Fighting 8th" (they had been a Civil War unit and then a division of the Illinois National Guard, but were incorporated into the segregated U.S. Infantry during World War I). We decided, black and white, that we had to see this. And as it turned out, on the very same night that show was happening, Joe Louis was fighting Jimmy Braddock for the heavyweight championship at nearby White Sox Park (Comiskey Park).

It was a big night, June 22, 1937. When we heard Joe had knocked Jim Braddock out, we all began to chant together in a sing-song:

> Joe Louis knocked Jim Braddock down
> Jim Braddock got right up and then
> Louis knocked him down again
> It makes no difference what you say
> The Champion is a [N——]!

A moment like that took the sting out of the N-word, and it became instead part of an ironic, sneering victory dance. We were simply elated.

In the vernacular of our day, the champion was indeed a Negro. And after the fight, Joe Louis and his entourage came across Thirty-Fifth Street to celebrate this win. And here we all were, a huge crowd, black and white, Jew and gentile, embracing one another and weeping. And Benny Goodman and his band played and sang "It Must Have Been Moonglow." Everybody danced. What a night.

Chicago was a hub of union organizing, and the musicians were no exception. Black musicians were subject to the same kind of racial discrimination as other black workers and tradespeople were. When big names came to play in the downtown Chicago hotels, they stayed in the Black Belt, often in the homes of friends and relatives in our neighborhood. As the saying went, they "could play downtown, but they couldn't stay downtown." The black musicians had to form their own musicians union. The Negro Musicians union hall was at Thirty-Eighth and

State, in the heart of our entertainment district. There are some who felt and still feel today that the two unions should never have merged, the way they eventually did. Jimmy Ellis, the great horn player from our neighborhood, always felt that the strength of their base was reduced substantially when they were merged, that the power of the black musicians was watered down. However, the musicians union played a tremendous part in spreading the music, breaking barriers in many places, and giving examples to other unions that then began to integrate.

Unionization helped break many of the barriers because blacks in the period of the black musicians union were restricted from playing north of Roosevelt Road, south of downtown Chicago. Roosevelt Road was like a DMZ. You couldn't cross it. When the unions merged, in 1966, that gave black musicians a new legitimacy. The hotels and the big downtown nightclubs had no choice. The union musicians would be able to play anywhere in the country, and eventually, in the world. The New York scene had always been more multiracial and cosmopolitan. But when the New York bands came to play in Chicago, they too had to respect and make a special agreement, a system which was finally broken when the two unions merged as the Chicago Federation of Musicians. Some members wanted to integrate and some didn't. Without a union card, you couldn't perform in public. You had to show your union card in order to work. The CFM became a very strong, powerful union, part of the American Federation of Musicians.

Accompanying the rise of jazz, we had a stream of dancers emerging from the community. And not only tap. We had classically trained ballet dancers and great ballroom dancers. There were Marie Bryant and sisters Mary and Sadie Bruce. And there was the inimitable Bill "Bojangles" Robinson. He performed frequently in Chicago and stayed in our neighborhood. When Bojangles came to town, he would give free dancing lessons to our young people. Marie Bryant was his student. She later became the choreographer for Duke Ellington's big, elaborate stage shows.

In the early 1930s, right at the outset of the Great Depression, Bojangles was in our neighborhood, offering lessons to some of our young dancers. He was in town for a performance at the Regal Theater. He had invented some new steps which he wanted to teach us, so we could dance to the rhythm of the jazz we were hearing.

I was not musically talented, and I couldn't dance. But one of the nice things about being dumb was that I had a lot of friends who wanted to make me smart. They wanted me to go with them to this dancing lesson with Mr. Robinson. Today I suppose you'd call it a master class. I was about thirteen years old, and there is nobody more awkward than a thirteen-year-old boy. Hard as I tried to learn to tap dance, I just didn't have any aptitude for it. Out of the whole group of us who were assembled to receive lessons from the master, it was soon evident that I was the only one who was not adept enough to tap.

So Mr. Robinson sent me over to the nearby hotel, where he and his wife were staying, to get him some tap shoes that he wanted. I ran this errand for him while all my friends took a lesson. When I got back with his shoes, he tipped me ten whole dollars. Understand how much money this was in 1930. This was maybe a couple weeks' worth of grocery money for our household. I could hardly believe my good fortune. I ran home shaking with excitement to turn that money over to Mama.

Another time, my buddies and I stood in the back of a theater on The Stroll hours before a show, watching the band set up. Sonny Greer was up there on the stage. Then this elegant man came out and began to play. He was sharp and cool. His name was Edward Kennedy Ellington, commonly called "Duke." My friends and I were moved. His sound was so symphonic in many ways, along with that jazz bounce. We were only eight, nine, ten years old, and we promised among ourselves he would never come to town without us seeing him.

We were good as our word. When Ellington came to town, we always went to see him. Many years after that first encounter, we were down in the basement at Louis Preer's house. It was our hang-out. Me and my best friends. The Preers were a prosperous family and owned a gambling joint. In their basement was a pool table where we worked on perfecting our game. We talked about life and girls, and we listened to music. It was 1940, just before the U.S. entered the war.

Duke was by now internationally renowned, but Duke could not play jazz in Germany or Austria. He and his company were denied entry, although they had been there before, earlier, and were popular. The Duke Ellington Orchestra was hugely popular throughout Europe. They had inspired the Hot Club of France, a fantastic jazz venue on the Left Bank. Of course, Josephine Baker had also played a pioneering role in popularizing jazz in Paris. Louis Armstrong and all those guys, many of them from Chicago, had been to Europe too, but they couldn't go to Germany. Wherever he visited Europe, Duke composed popular national jazz anthems, "Good Queen Bess" and "Song of Stockholm" and many more.

And then one time when he returned to the U.S., somebody ran into the Preer basement and announced that Duke was in town and that he was going to play in Chicago that very night, at a ballroom on the northwest side where blacks were not supposed to go.

But we had made our commitment years earlier. We looked at one another, and we said, "Let's go!" We were a big crowd. Maybe ten altogether, with our girlfriends. We jumped in the cars and got to the Marigold Room up at Broadway and Grace Street. At the ticket window, the clerk says, "Sorry, we're sold out." Now, we can plainly see that white customers are still buying tickets and going in. One of the girls said, "Tell Sonny Greer I'm out here." Sonny comes out and says, "What are you doing out here?" As if he didn't know. "Let me go get Duke," he says. So now the clerk has no standing. The manager comes out and explains to Duke that if we are let in, there is going to be a "riot." Duke says, "Well, these are my guests, and if they can't enjoy my performance, this show is over."

They put us at a couple of tables way back in the hall behind a curtain to partition us off from the white customers. We couldn't see the stage or the audience. Duke made them remove the curtain. Again, he says to the manager, "These are my guests, and if they can't enjoy my performance, this show is over." We didn't come there to dance or romance; we came to listen and to talk about the music, which we did, thanks to the great Duke Ellington. It turned out to be a glorious evening, a breakthrough in our relationship. It's one of the ways we began to bring about social justice and social change, the change that comes when people can share a common, enjoyable experience across racial, national, ethnic, and religious differences.

I was, after such experiences, alert to the spread of jazz around the world as an international phenomenon with roots in my own Sacred Ground. I was in Japan shortly after the end of World War II. Hiroshima was still a fresh memory. In a bar in Tokyo, I heard a young Japanese woman singing some stuff by Ella Fitzgerald. She was singing so well I assumed that she spoke English. So I went over to talk with her. But she had learned every note and syllable from records. She had sung in precisely that same style with a smile on her face, but she could not speak English. I found a translator. She was thrilled to learn that I had met

Ella Fitzgerald, and we bonded as we shared stories. She wanted to know more about Ella's background and personality.

Later I had occasion to visit Russia. It was post–World War II, and the Cold War was in full swing. I was in Moscow, and I was afraid to talk much politics. I wasn't talking about communism either pro or con. But one thing I could talk freely about was jazz music. We would talk about jazz music with glee. Count Basie and Ella Fitzgerald and all the big bands were traveling and performing as "goodwill ambassadors" throughout Asia and Europe, during and immediately after World War II. In many places they were the first blacks to visit in modern times.

Time and again I was carried by that music beyond the barriers and borders of the hostile world to a better world that might exist, that could open the gates, bring about friendship, sisterhood, brotherhood. Jazz was a universal part of the world culture. Besides the need for food, shelter, and clothing, we humans share a spiritual, non-materialistic need in our lives, and jazz carries those qualities of spirit and creative flow. It helps erode the barriers of segregation and discrimination, as we enjoy what each other has created.

As we walked and marched down the streets during the civil rights movement, even in Jackson or in Birmingham, even in those places, there was a bounce, there was a rhythm. As we sang there was the melody line. We created the feeling that somehow a change is gonna come, and so we brought about some of that change. The music buoyed us up. Of course, not enough has changed. But I have to believe that if we can continue to expand this cultural form that was born in New Orleans and refined in the city of Chicago, we will have made a contribution to humanity and the kind of world that should be.

Musicians were drafted into the military and made a great contribution during World War II. The biggest military base near Chicago was the Great Lakes Naval Base up in Waukegan. The Great Lakes Naval Band had a lot of our great black musicians. For instance, the great trumpeter Clark "Mumbles" Terry was there. This brought him to play in Chicago. Originally from St. Louis, Terry played with Count Basie and with the Ellington Orchestra in the 1940s and 1950s. He always wore his pants too short, sort of a trademark look. Somebody would say, "His shoes ought to have a party and invite his pants to come on down." You would never forget his performance of "Mumbles," or his rendition of the lyrics of "Porgy and Bess."

In the 1960s and on, a lot of the band programs in our public schools were closed out. We had some great jazz programs. In some of the more privileged schools, jazz is still part of the music curriculum. But this takes resources. Mostly it is only the elite, selective high schools and a few suburban high schools that still offer jazz education. Some of the most important high schools in the black community, where jazz instruction had its maturation, no longer have jazz. In my day, jazz was a huge motivational issue. As a youngster, I didn't play the music, but I wanted to get to school on time to *hear* the music. The music stimulated me to do better even in all my non-musical classes. So, unconsciously, it had a positive effect even on me, a non-musician. I have bragged that I went to school with Nat Cole. But I had to do well in school myself in order to brag. Jazz, and music in general, certainly leavens not only the atmosphere in a school, but at a subconscious level, it deepens the learning process. Jazz music in particular—and contemporary brain research seems to confirm this—embeds an awareness of these beats, of this system of ratio and proportion. How are you going to know all these beats without recognizing a little math? There are so many other stimuli embedded in jazz that you begin to be a little more engaged, a little more alert. For me, music helped to carry me through adolescence, attracting me to school and increasing the joy and the fun of it.

That's why, for the past few decades, I've worked on the board of the Jazz Institute of Chicago. My focus has been on preserving Chicago's unique jazz heritage and reinstating it in our high schools, not just by exposing young people to jazz through one-time experiences, but by building and enshrining jazz education programs and partnerships in our high schools for the long term.

We grew up immersed in and surrounded by the music. Jazz and music were one and the same. We don't hear it today as we once did. And our young people certainly don't. There is no jazz radio station in Chicago, while once there were many. It was everywhere. My mother played it. You don't grow up wanting to play what you do not hear. For older generations, the desire to play was cultivated almost like osmosis, like you learn a language. It's in the air. But no longer. In my younger years, I couldn't help but get it. The music was all around. We didn't have air-conditioning in those days. Much of the year, the windows were open, and you could hear music streaming from the houses.

When I was teaching, one of the ways I used to fascinate kids was to play them some Grappelli and Reinhardt, from the Hot Club in France. "Listen with me. They're playin' our music in their way." It strikes a spirit of curiosity in youngsters that they can then take what the old man has offered. They'd go home and look through their parents' music collection, and come back and tell me, "Oh, Mr. Black, look what I found," because the parents and grandparents, whether they played it or not, still had some of those old jazz classics in the house.

My hope and dream is that if we do this long enough, it will serve our ultimate mission of social justice and unity. We have these young men with all the tools of destruction, but music can serve them as tools of mass *construction*. I want them to have the gift that raised me and my friends up, that carries with it love and affection and a beat that encompasses hopes and dreams. You may call this a fantasy at this moment in our history. But it's been my fantasy, probably since I left Birmingham at eight months of age, that when I got to Chicago, it was gonna be a better world. We're not completely there yet, but we are certainly a lot further along thanks to our shared dream. That may sound simplistic, but at my advanced age, that part of my vision carries me forward and invigorates me. When I go home tonight I'll do my own jazz set while consuming a little glass of merlot. I put on a record and play like I'm in a jazz set with friends. I can get to sleep more peacefully to the rhythm. I snap my fingers and tap my feet and shake a little bit. Tomorrow will be better. The music carries that spirit of believing and knowing that tomorrow will be a better day, but we must *make* it a better day not just for ourselves but for others, and share the beauty of life, not just the booty of life. I've been lucky to physically survive to this ripe old age and to remain twenty-three in my heart.

So now our challenge is how to broaden this desire for music, and specifically for jazz, across gender lines, generational lines, racial lines, so that somewhere we embrace this universality, this common spirituality of joy with that African beat and that European melody line that affirms we are all sharing this earth together and that there is no monopoly on joy.

CHAPTER 3

Soldiering On

The impossible—we do that immediately;
the miraculous may take a little longer.

—ARMY SERVICE FORCES

Part 1—The Impossible

As I said, I was inducted into the army in August of 1943. My first draft notice had said something like, "Greetings, you have been selected from among your neighbors to serve Uncle Sam." And I sent it back saying, "I don't have an uncle named Sam. My uncles are named William and Walter." But they sent me another one and my mama said, "You'd better go."

I was sent to Camp Custer in Wisconsin for assignment in September, and from there we went for basic training to Camp Lee, Virginia, which is right outside the town of Petersburg, Virginia.

Some of us would have done pretty well on the Army General Classification Test (AGCT). This was a placement test, and those who scored high were put aside to go to the Officer Candidate School. But we were in all black training companies, under white officers. We had black noncommissioned officers, but all of our officers were white, regardless of how well you may have done on the AGCT. Generally speaking, with relatively minor exceptions, the highest rank a black soldier could attain would be master sergeant, something of that nature. In all black units, there were a few who became officers, but none were over any white troops.

My brother was in the army too, a master sergeant, though he should have been an officer, and one day I decided to go visit him and his wife down in Durham, North Carolina, where Camp Butner was. So I got on the streetcar to go to the train that went to Durham from Richmond, Virginia, and the driver didn't say anything because I was the only person on the streetcar. But then he picks up some more passengers and tells me I'm sitting in the wrong seat and need to move. I thought to myself, "Well, it's time to die." I had a lot of my daddy's attitude. The driver says that I should be sitting in the back and I say, "Why didn't you tell me that when I first got on. If it didn't matter then it doesn't matter now." Fortunately, we were by the train station, and I got off to get on the train. I was in my uniform and getting ready to go fight for these people, and I was not about to move.

I was at Camp Lee for about three months, and we thought we would be going overseas soon. I went home on leave and had a good time, but then I was sent to a camp in Pennsylvania. My friend Travis went to that same camp. He and some of his fellow soldiers were fired on when they tried to go off base to a movie. He was shot and disabled, and was almost killed. Two of the fellows were killed by the military police because they tried to go to this theater, which was off limits to black troops. There are many more sworn accounts of similar incidents that happened to black GIs during that period all over the country. But this particular incident occurred right near Pittsburgh, and it happened to guys stationed at the same camp as me.

From there we learned that we were going to go overseas. I was very much against being in the army at that point, not only because of the abuse within the military, but more generally. There was a race riot in Detroit just before I was inducted, and another in New York. My daddy's position was, "Why are you going to go over there and fighting when you should be going up to Detroit and fighting those battles?" It was hard to argue with his logic.

My mama, of course, was just as strong for justice as my daddy was, but much more conscious of what that might mean in terms of my future, and so she insisted that I go into the army. She said, "You go there, and you come back with an honorable discharge." I think it's fair to say that most black folks were more than a little conflicted about joining the army, given all the built-in inequalities and the violence directed against us even in northern cities. But there were bigger fish to fry. Even so, there were undertones of fear. It was rumored that one of our contemporaries, somebody in the neighborhood, someone around our age, had actually committed suicide to avoid induction into the army. But such things were talked about quietly.

At that time my parents also had to deal with some sadness, the death of my older sister, Charlotte. She had gone to Crane Junior College and married the son of a Rev. Washington, and they had a son, Tyree. But it was not a happy marriage, and my sister ended up being very troubled. Her husband died prematurely, and she never got over that, going off to live alone while we took Tyree into our house. He was like a little brother to me. He worked as an usher at the Regal—and would let me in for free—and then worked for the railroad. But my sister was devastated and never really recovered.

When we got into World War II, many of the blacks of draft age were already married and had children, and so were not going to be selectees. So the black men from Chicago who went into the army were mostly single. Besides those black men like me who were drafted, there were many who volunteered, including a good many of my friends. Some of them were in the acclaimed Tuskegee Airmen. They were loyal Americans, and they also wanted to learn to fly, to become officers, to win recognition for black Americans. This was not the first such instance in our history. We decided we had to be good soldiers. We had to come out with an honorable discharge and take whatever assignments we had seriously and become good soldiers.

Many of my friends who were in combat units wanted to go and fight against the Japanese or the Germans. Those who did not want to be in combat units—and some of those who did want to be in combat units—were assigned to service units, like the quartermasters corps, the engineers, or communications and the like, rather than actual confrontational combat. However, the combat troops could not do anything without these service units. And so we had to be close to them all the time in order to get them the necessary services—food, shelter, ammunition, and other forms of support and supplies. It was neither safe nor easy duty, as I soon discovered.

We moved on to New Jersey, to the base camp of departure for overseas. We shipped out and went the roundabout way to the British Isles, touching land in Scotland, and finally winding up in Wales, where we continued our training. The local people where we were in Wales had never seen any blacks; they thought that we had just stayed out in the sun too long! But some of them had been informed by the white soldiers that we were like dogs and had tails, and that we were not quite human. So they were curious about us. They came to find that we were very human; the young ladies in particular found that out rather quickly. We were exceedingly popular.

I was assigned to the 308 Quartermasters Corps, the Quartermaster Railhead Company. We received intensive, rigorous training. We didn't quite know what for. Then one night we were all put on these six-by-six trucks, and we wound up in a town near London, where we were locked in with watchdogs and guards all around. We didn't know what was going on. We were held there for a couple of days, and on June 6, 1944, we learned that Americans had gone into France. My unit was supposed to go in, on D-Day, June 6. We were supposed to go in, but my commander and the commander of the 307th wanted to challenge each other as to who would go in with their troops first, and the other guy won. That unit went in that day and was practically wiped out. I was glad not to have been there, to tell the truth.

They went into what they called the Hot Beach—Omaha—and they were slaughtered. My unit went in about four days later. We waded through the water to Utah Beach, and that's how I got to France. "Utah" was another sector of Normandy Beach, and there were land mines all over the place. The Germans had planted them lavishly. But the commander of that sector was a relative of Theodore Roosevelt, and he was determined to plow through. He said, "You standing down here on the beach and getting killed. Let's go inland and get killed." So they commanded us to move in. And then when we got up to Ste.-Mère-Église, a small community near the beach, we were welcomed by the French people. I was amazed. I had a chance to utilize my schoolboy French, which was better than that of our interpreter. We had a young man from Louisiana in our unit, and he could deal with patois and the variations in the linguistic style of people down there.

Dead animals were lying in the fields, and yet people were out hanging up their laundry. There were land mines, bombs were bursting around us, and yet they went on doing their daily chores. There was a sort of fatalism, as if whatever is going to happen is going to happen and we may as well keep things going. We were encamped there near the beach, and every so often a German plane would come in and dive and strafe us. They would fire on our trucks. We called our supply trucks the Red Ball Express.

The Germans dropped a bomb on one of our ammunition dumps, and the command ordered that the service troops had to go in and isolate the live ammunition from exploding ammunition. This was one of the most perilous duties. That's really cannon fodder. They disproportionately chose black troops for this duty. You were between a rock and a hard place. If you refused, you would be cited for disobeying your commander's orders. But there were those who did refuse to do it—they did not receive their honorable discharges. Some ventured in and did it, and some of them were wiped out in that process.

General George Patton, commander of the Third Army, arrived and took charge. Patton wanted to move very swiftly up toward Belgium. One of my cousins, who was in the engineer corps, helped to bring sea water down to the lines. They used sea water when they couldn't get fresh. We happened to bump into each other there, on the other side of the ocean, in the midst of carnage. And my cousin told me, "Whatever you do, don't get captured, because the Germans are not taking any Negroes." Meaning "they're not taking any blacks alive. So since you might die that way anyhow, just die fighting, protecting yourself." We were forewarned.

The German sharpshooters were sniping, trying to pick off the officers. They knew that the guy who had the stripe on his helmet was the leader, and they figured that if they could kill the leader, then the other troops would fall into disarray. What the Germans didn't understand about the American system though, was that the leader might have been a worker, while the lowest-ranking guy in the company may be the multimillionaire. The commanding officer, of course, had a higher score on the management test, but that test wasn't based on economic or class status. When somebody would knock off the captain or the major, someone else who had managerial experience might just step in and take charge, because they had experience doing that. Still, it became necessary to remove those stripes from the backs of the helmets for the noncommissioned and commissioned officers so that they could not be so easily singled out.

We had to move along with the trucks, since Patton wanted to push north and we had to move the necessary supplies. He wanted us to be up there waiting for the supplies as they came, as they were being dumped on the beaches. The Red Ball Express drivers, now, those guys were fabulous. The trucks weren't actually going that fast, but those guys could drive in all different positions. The Germans would be shooting at our trucks, trying to hit the drivers, and we had drivers who could stand outside on the running board while the truck was rolling, and keep it under control even while being fired on. They were so adept. They were exceptional guys. We had a job to do, and we wanted to get back home. So being careful was one thing, but doing your job was the main priority. So many were depending on us.

At one point, we were surrounded by the Germans while moving up toward Paris. Patton issued an invitation that anyone who wanted to be in the combat unit could do so, whatever his race, creed, or religion. We had some young guys in our unit—eighteen-, nineteen-year-old adventurous young men who volunteered to do that, but I said, "Not me. I'm going to be right where I am." By this time I'm about twenty-five years old. I had seen a few people die. So I could see what death was like, and I wanted no part of it.

Some of these young men had prison records, and they were motivated; they wanted to get discharged with honors and medals so they could go back home with a good record and make a new start. A lot of the fellows in my unit were from rural Arkansas and Mississippi. There were a few of us city boys. Leon Dash, for example, was from New York. I was from Chicago, of course, and we had a number of guys from places like Detroit, New York, and New Orleans, though these were sometimes soldiers from other units. There was a distinct tension between the urban fellows and the rural agricultural fellows. We had to get over that. They thought we thought we were better than them. And maybe we did. But one of the things they had that we didn't have was that they knew how to shoot. In those days city kids did not grow up around guns. But the country boys knew how to shoot because they'd grown up hunting for food.

And they learned languages very quickly—they picked up French, Flemish, German, because of course it facilitated communication with the local young women. Now, if a young French girl or a young British girl was sixteen years of age she might consent to have a love affair with a young man who was eighteen. There were affairs between young soldiers and young local women all the time, but if there happened to be a relationship between a black soldier and a white woman in those countries, that was forbidden and the pressure could be intense. If that happened with a black soldier, the girl would have to testify against him sometimes—she would have to testify against him because of the threat of penalty. With the breadbasket of the whole war at their disposal, the authorities could withdraw the supplies from her town, from her family. Or from the entire community.

The pressure of that kind of threat was overpowering. The girl might even be in love with this young man. He might likewise have affection for her. They might do what young men and young women do when they feel that way. But it was forbidden between a black and a white: it was not to be. So we had young men in our unit who were arrested and incarcerated, who were accused and found guilty of those false charges—of rape. Black soldiers were incarcerated, and some went before a firing squad in these instances. Those sitting in judgment on them were white officers, generally from the South.

It happened to me, though I was not in such a relationship. We were in combat, heading up to Belgium, when I was framed—I was number 10 in a lineup of black soldiers, and the girl was instructed by the white officers to pick me out, to pick out number 10, and accuse me of rape. She did, and I was put in the military prison for a couple of days. It was terrible, but fortunately for me, I had not even been in town the night of my supposed crime, and I was cleared when the girl could not identify me in another lineup.

The racism that existed was so blatant. It helped some when General Benjamin Oliver Davis Sr., the first black Brigadier General, was doing his inspection tours of the black soldiers in the army, but it was still a pervasive problem. When Eisenhower became the Supreme Allied Commander of the Allied Expeditionary Force (SHAEF), he tried to solve that racial problem. That turned some of his own officers against him.

General Eisenhower did at least try to solve this problem of intense confrontation, particularly in the towns and cities of Great Britain. He ordered that specific units be assigned to particular cities or towns. But the nicest cities and towns were given to the white troops, and those that no one wanted to go to were given to the Negro troops. There was resistance against that, as the black troops felt that they were being mistreated. They would go into the town as ordered, and soon you would have another [racial] confrontation with British civilians, although many of Britain's own troops were colonials recruited from British or French colonies in Africa, south Asia, and the Caribbean. They did not have the racial problems in the islands that we had in the United States. They wondered why we had two armies, one black and one white, and they asked that question. They made note that the white troops had no black officers over them, but the black troops, by and large, except for those who were from the National Guard, like the Fighting 8th or something like that, had all white officers. Some of the black units in the Ninety-Second Division, for example, had black commissioned officers. But the black troops, regardless of their qualifications or degree of educational attainment—and we had many highly educated men among us—were primarily commanded by some white guy who may have just barely graduated from high school.

So that created a social clash and resentment. I certainly felt angry about having to obey an officer who had control of my life, but who I felt was not smarter than me. He sensed that I knew that, so he tried to keep me in my place. He had to do things to remind me, like not promoting me although I was doing the work. He promoted others who, he felt, did not resent or challenge him.

Fortunately, I had some skills that were needed. But I had to be very careful about my own temper, which was true of many of us undergoing this kind of stress. When we were in the Battle of the Bulge, it became evident that the air corps got privileges that the other troops did not get. They could just come in and ask us quartermasters for whatever they wanted. We were outside the town of Bruges, in Belgium. The trucks would come in, and we would get our supplies. There was a Jewish guy from New York in charge of the pick-up unit. He was a nice guy. He would always bring us some kind of alcohol because the air corps had all these privileges, and he would be apologetic, explaining to us that he couldn't get gin or bourbon. It was catch-as-catch-can, but we were always glad to get it. Another soldier in the unit saw the privileges that we were according this Jewish leader and his unit. These guys were air corps, and they were going to get whatever they wanted regardless of ethnicity. This other soldier, who was not Jewish, muttered to me, "Hitler was right." I replied, "I don't know what you came in here looking for, but whatever it is, we just ran out of it." If he could say such a thing about the Jews, he obviously could and would say the same thing about the "n——s." Then he tried to get me in trouble, complaining to my commander. But without me and the other supply troops, our commander wouldn't be able to do anything. So he just said, "Private Black is in charge."

The Worst of Times

In 1944, we were young men going up into Paris, going up into northern France under General Patton. We were moving faster than our supplies. Finally, our trucks and everything caught up and at one point, we were supplying, on a daily basis, hundreds of thousands of troops with the necessities in terms of food and *equipage*, as they called it—equipment, military materiel, and ammunition. We had carbine rifles rather than the M1 Garands, which were used in combat. We had to keep our weapons handy because at any point we might run into trouble, which we did.

When we got near Paris, the French Forces of the Interior—with whom Jean-Paul Sartre served as a sergeant—asked us to wait. They wanted us to stay outside Paris until they symbolically liberated Paris. And when we came into Paris, we marched down the Champs Elysees. General de Gaulle had come back from England, where he had been in exile, and we marched down the liberated Champs Elysees. That was a great day—August 26, 1944. The French, who had remained hopeful after so many years of occupation and betrayal by some of their own citizens, some of their own leaders, they were saying, "Vive la France, vive l'Amerique, vive le Russe," and as the black troops passed they waved jazz records! They yelled out "Louis Armstrong!" when they saw us. They were mad about the Hot Club of France, Django Reinhardt, and Stéphane Grappelli—the guitar player and the violinist, you know, they had the Quintet of the Hot Club of France. Louis Armstrong and Bennie Carter and other black American jazz greats had played with them before the war at the exclusive clubs. So they had kept those records, and they wanted to wave them to show their support.

We went through France, went through Paris, and then up into Belgium. We liaised, stopping in Luxembourg sometime early in 1945, but just before the holidays in 1944 we fought the Battle of the Bulge. The German oil supplies had been destroyed by our American planes, particularly where the oil fields were. So although they had planes, the

Germans couldn't get many of them off the ground. They didn't have the fuel. Our commanding officer's tactical plan was to destroy the supply lines. Now, this is the same thing that Napoleon and others had done earlier, or had done to them. The Russians had done that when the Germans were going into central Prussia, which was by this time part of the Soviet Union. So our aims were to cut the supply lines and blow up the bridges, and that put us directly in the area of combat.

We had a bunch of captured Germans, prisoners of war, and we had to bring them with us, and we chose to treat them humanely, by which I mean, we had to treat them like human beings. They were captured, and they were glad to no longer be on the front line. The Germans we had captured would almost invariably ask, "When are the Americans and the Russians going to start their fight?" Almost everyone assumed that a war between Russia and the U.S. would be next. It was seen as inevitable.

They told us that some of the British ranks had been infiltrated by younger SS guys who spoke perfect English. Some of these younger Germans had actually lived in the U.S. or in England. Their mission was to blow up the supplies from the inside, while the planes were left to blow up bridges. What this meant was that we had to confine all of those German prisoners and keep them out of action. The orders to our unit were to capture any white person that we saw out after dark, either capture them or kill them, any white person. That was the order. We couldn't trust them just because they spoke English. They knew American habits. You could ask them, you know, what the New York Yankees did. They could tell you pretty accurately. So that wouldn't flush them out.

We had our orders. It was a critical moment in the war in Europe. We knew that the Germans had developed, but not perfected, missiles. Often the missiles would go awry because they didn't have any direction. So they would just fire them and, of course, our ranks were sometimes victimized by those. The Germans were trying to get them into France and into England, into London in particular. So we were constantly alert, and getting any sleep was out.

The Battle of the Bulge was horrific. We fought through the Ardennes Forest, dragging the prisoners with us. We finally came to a breaking point. In the combat zone, all the rules break down. You can't afford any of them. The commanders pulled the veterans, the most seasoned soldiers, off of the front line and replaced them with young men who had just been drafted or volunteered from the States—eighteen-, nineteen-year-olds were sent up to be cannon fodder. They were expendable. But we were also expendable, and so that was quite an experience. Not one I would want to repeat.

During that period of time we were always ambivalent, even my commanding officer, for we heard that the German troops were surrendering in large numbers. We felt the tide was turning. And the combat troops whom we armed and supplied were winning. The Battle of the Bulge was practically over and won. But we had heard there were some awful things that our combat soldiers had seen in parts of Germany. We wanted to go and see for ourselves. They had seen the concentration camps, which they had liberated. And even though most of them had seen violence and had been in combat, they had not witnessed anything like that. The concentration camps were beyond our imagination.

We were moving from Belgium into Germany, and we wanted to see what the combat soldiers were talking about. So we got into the jeep—I went with my commanding officer, even though we were not friendly— and we drove up into a town called Buchenwald. As we got closer, you could smell a smell and hear these cries. It was barely recognizable as human. Nowhere had I encountered anything like that smell or that sound. When we reached the camp, we saw these creatures that seemed to be human beings, but starved humans. You could actually see their whole skeletons. Their skin had become transparent. This place was organized so that all the gold, all the precious metals were very carefully taken from the bodies and catalogued. The camp was inhabited by mostly Jews and "Gypsies" (the Roma), as well as affluent German intellectuals and gay men, but mostly the Jews and the Roma. They all reached up to us, as if to beg for anything to eat. More and more of them emerged from the barracks. I was so hurt, so angry, that I began to cry, and my first priority was to kill all the Germans. I was just overwhelmed.

We asked people in the town how they could let something like this happen, and they said "Mister, it was the Führer." They would not take responsibility, even though they had run the place.

Then I began to realize that some of our soldiers were of German descent—even Eisenhower, Eichelberger, you can go on and name them. This got me to reflecting, and I thought, this can happen anywhere to anyone.

By this time I had survived the worst of the battles. I was now very cautious about my own fellow soldiers, because they would play around with guns. Sometimes they would shoot at each other, just good friends playing around with weapons. So I was more afraid of them by this time than I was of anything else. I had even begun to relax, believing that maybe I was going to get back home. But I had one period when I didn't believe I was going to make it, where had it not been for a guy on the truck with me, I would have just jumped off the truck and then been crushed by the truck right behind. That was just a very brief period of intense depression, when I wondered "What the hell am I living for?"

When the Germans had bombed out the trains that had the mail on them, my mind went a funny way. My mama, like many mothers and sweethearts and wives, wrote a letter every day. And now we weren't getting mail. I began to doubt that my parents were alive. Of course, all of our mail was censored. But I got an irrational, complex feeling, blaming my mother and father for not keeping in touch with me. This kind of misdirected anger comes from extreme stress. You need someone to blame. I was doubly confused because I knew that if there was any way possible, Mama was going to get a letter to me. Therefore, there must be something wrong with them. Then my anger would rise up at them for forsaking me. Luckily for my sanity, my mother got to the Red Cross and got a message to me. I sent a message back. When she got that message from the Red Cross, she felt certain: "My baby, he is all right. He is going to be all right. God is going to take care of him." And when I got that message from her I thought "It's going to be all right." I remembered how my farsighted mama had said to me, when I left home, "You go there and you come back with an honorable discharge." I tried to remember that every time I wondered what the hell I was living for.

Now anyone who has been in combat or close to combat will understand that. You get confused. You can be very irrational. That's why still today we always have to worry about these kids coming back from war. They volunteered; we didn't in most instances. But either way, war takes a terrible toll.

The confusions that arose in me in that period of time were so great because I was alone a great deal. I didn't have anyone with whom to talk about what I had seen. I wasn't a gambler. I wouldn't play with the guys sometimes when they would play some poker or some other game to get some relief. I would be by myself a lot of the time, too much of the time. Seeing Buchenwald, the death camp, changed me. The death camp. The only ones who didn't die there were the ones who were liberated because of the arrival of the American and Russian troops. I felt like I had been given a second life. And I determined that when I returned home I was going to spend the rest of my life working for peace and justice. That was a commitment to myself. To the extent that I could keep it, I've tried. I've done my best.

Our unit was eventually sent to Marseilles, France, the big port. We were getting ready to go home. For our service rendered from the Normandy Invasion through the Battle of the Bulge, my whole unit was awarded the Croix de Guerre with Palm. Although the French government gave my unit a major award, the Croix de Guerre with Palm, we were not similarly honored by the United States Army, though I did earn four Bronze Battle Stars. The French Army appreciated our service so much because down on the beach, in that rain of fire, we saved the supplies. We moved the supplies up through France into Belgium. Without those supplies there would have been no victories, because the German field marshall Gerd Von Rundstedt wanted to encircle our troops, using and destroying the supplies. We were attacked as often as the combat troops.

The intentions were that next we would sail to Japan, to take over Japan with the troops that were already in the Far East. But while in Marseilles, on the sixth of August, 1945, we learned that the Americans had dropped a weapon on Japan that was like nothing we had ever imagined.

I had been in London when bombs went off in London. I'd seen the destruction they caused. I had been in the European theater. But I couldn't imagine something that was the size of a golf ball inside a bigger piece of metal that could immediately kill almost 100,000 people in a place called Hiroshima and then three days later, another one in Nagasaki. I expressed the idea to my fellow soldiers that I would have preferred to have gone to Japan and taken my chances than for us to have done that to two cities full of people. These cities were not major military targets. The people had little or no warning. Not that a warning could have saved them. I would have preferred to go and fight it out hand to hand than to roast human beings like that. That feeling still has me now. We gave the entire world the example of what we now call a preemptive strike. How can we say that some other country should not do the same thing to us, if they assume that this is the way? That was not a popular thought. I said it to my fellow soldiers.

I was about twenty-six years old by this time, going on twenty-seven. I was a man. We were getting ready to come home. The war was over. Some young white soldiers were assigned to our ship. They had just arrived in France, and yet they were given the opportunity to board that ship. We black troops were taken off and reassigned. A young white soldier said to me, "You mean to tell me you are going to let them take you off that ship?" And it was amazing to me for him to say that. You gonna let them do that to you? An expression of fairness. Was it amazing that a white person could see the injustice? Or that he would have the nerve to criticize me for going along with it? Anyway, I should have said, "Oh, no, I wouldn't let that happen." But in my shame, I said to him, "See, you don't understand. You are not a Negro." They were right. There were just so many incidents like that.

Some of my most persistent memories of the war are about these kinds of little incidents and insults, about how the divisions between people can cause them to try to divide other people. So when I am listening to this young soldier saying, "You mean that you are going to let them take you off that ship?" I had to explain it to him. His feelings were: "You are an American. You have served your country. You have been in more danger than I have been in, and I'm going to go home and you can't go home, and that is not right." That was his attitude. He was absolutely right. He was letting me know that he saw the unfairness.

Of course, I do also have some pleasant memories of those times. I enjoyed the pleasures of my brief time in Paris. That is classified information.

Finally, we did get on a ship and we sailed on home. We approached the New York harbor and there's the Statue of Liberty, and there are mostly white soldiers up on deck crying and yelling, "There she is, that old devil, that old bitch . . ." I was determined, because I was so angry, that I was not going to do that. But I found myself going up on the deck and crying with the rest of them. I was crying with joy and relief and appreciation. It's that conundrum, that paradox that has come up on a number of occasions in my life. When I was asked by a Frenchman or a German or whoever, "How can you be fighting for and so loyal to a country that mistreats you?" I would quickly respond, "That is none of your business. I am an American. We will straighten that out when we get home. But that is none of your business."

The ambivalence of our feelings was real and was shared by many, and it is still shared by many. Yes, our feelings for America are conflicted, but there is a loyalty that overrides the conflict. I wept, and a soldier friend of mine from upstate New York said to me, "When we get back home, we are going to organize so that never again will there be a segregated army." Now, that was a big thing for us to be thinking about.

We kept in touch with one another. The relationships forged in the army among black troops reappeared in the civil rights movement. Our history of service gave us credentials. Our patriotism had been tested. We got back home, and we took the Illinois Central. We stopped at the Twelfth Street Station. It was Christmas day of 1945. We came in and reported to Camp Grant, and waited to be discharged. I was with a light-skinned friend of mine, a guy who really looked white, although he was very black. I told him, "For the first time I'm going AWOL." I was supposed to be discharged two days later, but it was Christmas 1945. So we got on the street car and went to 6230 South Vernon. There were my mother and father, having Christmas dinner with some friends. My mama heard my key in the door and she knew. She said, "That's my baby." I stayed overnight and then reported back to camp in northeast Illinois.

But anyway, we went back to get a discharge. They asked my buddy if he wanted to continue to be in the army, and he said, "Yes." But when they asked me, I said, "I wouldn't even join the Salvation Army. Give me my discharge." They gave me that piece of paper. I had come home with the determination to fight on the home front. Now, my buddy stayed in and I think he served in Korea, and he was later killed on the road.

When we came out of the army, the army was still very segregated. But from that point on, no longer would there be such a segregated army. The process was accelerated by the formation of the Progressive Party in 1948. Henry A. Wallace from Iowa, who had served as secretary of agriculture and then as FDR's vice president and then as secretary of commerce, was running for president. There was never a more experienced or highly qualified presidential candidate. My old high school friend from DuSable, activist Clarice Durham, recalls how "we both attended the 1948 Founding Convention of the Progressive Party in Philadelphia. He [Tim] was a Delegate and I was an Observer. We worked in the presidential campaign of Henry Wallace, on a platform of ending segregation, ensuring full voting rights for Blacks, and providing universal government health insurance."

But the Democrats rejected Henry Wallace because he was too liberal, even though he had been a vice president. Truman was running for president as the candidate of the Democratic Party (it was Truman who gave the go-ahead to drop the bomb in 1945). Strom Thurmond was also running, as the Dixiecrat arch-segregationist, and Thomas Dewey was running as the Republican candidate. Truman won, and even though he was not as liberal as Wallace, in 1948 he issued Executive Order 9981, banning racial discrimination in the U.S. Armed Forces. But the work of desegregation would take time.

And by the way, the influence of Roosevelt was so universal that when he died suddenly in 1945, a woman in Liège, Belgium, came up to me and said, "Monsieur, le president des Etats-Unis est mort; qu'est-ce que nous allons faire?" ("The President of the United States is dead; what are we going to do?") That was the affection that people had for FDR. He was universally loved, because he had a quality so different than one of oppression. I'm not saying he was a perfect person, but that's how great his influence was.

Now of course, in 1945 and 1946, when most of us arrived home, we arrived to segregated communities, segregated jobs. Racial segregation was as epidemic as it had been when we left. We had decided, many of us, not to accept it any longer. And not just blacks, but whites and Latinos, Puerto Ricans and the Japanese, who had been incarcerated without any compensation (and by the way, their unit in Italy was the most decorated in the whole United States Army). It was the beginning of something new.

Part 2—The Miraculous

I believe that it was General Eisenhower who during the war would echo a popular motto from groups like the Army Service Forces: "The impossible—we do that immediately; the miraculous may take a little longer."

The things we once imagined were impossible only *became* possible because people continued to struggle to *make* them possible. Of course, that was true for Eisenhower too. He couldn't have done the impossible without *us*! That applies to social change, right up to the election of America's first black president: Everything we did laid the groundwork for the impossible—maybe even the miraculous—to be achieved. That's part of the American contradiction. Can we have democracy? No. It's impossible. No, but it's desirable. No, we don't need it. We got a million nos thrown up at us. But we can never give up—we can do the impossible.

Everyone who fought in the Second World War, and I'm sure in every other war, came back filled with trauma. It was not considered manly to talk about it. We often suffered in silence, from the anxiety, the racism, the mental and emotional as well as physical wounds. Some people came back and had great difficulty finding their footing in civilian life. Some took to drink.

In my case, political activism and organizing was the key to recovering from the whole deeply difficult experience of war. You never forget war, and you never get fully away from it.

Those of us black GIs who served in Europe in the Second World War were confronted and reproached by people in the places we went—in France, in England, in Germany—who were critical of the U.S. We were not always the most beloved country; we were just the richest country. Others wanted to get what we had in terms of economics. Again, people would call attention to the fact that they saw white officers over Negro troops, but never the reverse. Despite my sharp awareness of the inequities in the military, I felt defensive and protective of the U.S. when faced with these observations from Europeans. I deeply wanted "my" country to be better, fairer, and more respected. That was the fight I volunteered for, after the war.

When we returned from the war, we also found profound changes on the home front. Prior to World War II, women, whether black or white, seldom worked outside the home. Before that period, a woman wearing pants would be considered almost obscene. Now it was convenient. The women began to borrow and alter men's pants. A whole new style of dress began, and at the same time, women began, sometimes, to make as much money as the men. This began to set new rules for relationships. Families began to change, slowly.

The demise of the traditional family accelerated more rapidly in the black community, as women became able to do without men, without realizing what the impact would be on the family. With the second Great Migration, many industrial jobs began to go away. The conscious theme of equality did not emerge in the culture as fast as the civil rights movement tried to position it, and the civil rights movement did not put a great deal of emphasis on women. That was a problem.

The attitude of guys like me and the families of people like mine was to make a better life for ourselves and others. And we joined with whites to help do that, men and women, but the women did not get enough credit. My own family life was changing.

During the prewar period I had met my first wife to be, Norisea. We met through a mutual friend who was also an agent for the Metropolitan Funeral System. We were all street agents. We actually canvassed people on the streets. The giant (white-owned) Metropolitan Life Insurance Company claimed we were stealing business from them by using their name. It went to court, and eventually the name of our employer had to be changed from the Metropolitan Funeral System to the Metropolitan Mutual Assurance Company, Inc. Norisea was younger than me—she was nineteen and I was twenty-eight—and she wanted to get married. She was born and reared in Chicago; the family had come to Chicago back in 1893. They lived on the northernmost end of the Black Belt. Norisea's mother and others lived close by (her parents had divorced, which was unusual in those days). Norisea was a very bright girl. We married in 1946. Her maiden name was Norisea Cummings, and we had two children together—Ermetra and Timuel Kerrigan Black, born in 1947 and 1953. We all lived with my parents.

I had gone back to work for the Metropolitan Mutual Assurance Company after the war, but was soon fired for trying to organize the agents. They were looking for a way to get rid of me. They examined my books and found shortages, which was not unusual. We often let customers slide for a payment or two, in order to keep them as customers. But they were out to get me, and I was out of work. So that is why I had to go back to school, just as Mama wanted me to. I was able to take advantage of the GI Bill of Rights to get myself enrolled at Roosevelt University. I even convinced Norisea to go back to night school and finish at Englewood High School, but she was not confident about school. I kept going, registering at Roosevelt University and later at the University of Chicago. Pretty soon the social distance between us increased. When I was at the University of Chicago, white girls would tell her how nice her husband was. I continued to move along and she didn't. We separated, and finally she asked for a divorce. But we always took good care of our children. I will talk more about them later in this book, when I can brag some.

But by that time, the late fifties, I had become tremendously active in the civil rights movement, and I was demand all over the country. There were few black accredited anthropologists or sociologists. They could put the real test as to whether race matters. But my political education is a longer story, and I need to back up a bit.

There was always a relationship between blacks and progressive whites, particularly among people in my generation. I had been organizing since high school, and I had already been part of the early civil rights movement, even before I went off to the army. CORE, the Congress of Racial Equality, was cofounded in 1942 on the South Side of Chicago by James Farmer, who had worked with the Fellowship of Reconciliation, and it was dedicated to ending segregation through nonviolence. Farmer worked with people like George Houser, Bernice Fisher, Homer Jack, and Jim Robinson, who was a student at the University of Chicago. Bernice Fisher helped develop the tactic of sitting in at restaurants. They were all Gandhians long before King, and followed the principles set out in Krishnalal Shridharani's *War without Violence*.

I had a few friends at our A.M.E. Church at Sixty-Fourth and Evans, which was led by the Reverend Archibald Carey Jr., whose father had been pastor at Quinn Chapel, and who was a big supporter of CORE. During and after World War II, many of those young men and women became socially and politically active, and the idea of CORE was to break down discrimination in jobs, downtown and even in Hyde Park. They began to picket, protest, and sit in at all sorts of places—the Jack Spratt Coffee Shop, the White City Roller Rink, and others. I liked what was happening, but my friends and I were often political in other ways.

In the early forties, before the war, we had two major pool halls in the area, and also out in Washington Park. They were gathering spots for the young men. The daddies saw to it that the owners of the pool halls protected their kids. Dad's Very Safe Pool Hall at Fifty-First and Indiana was *almost* exclusively for young men under eighteen. Bill "Bojangles" Robinson, who was a frequent visitor to the Jones brothers, known as the policy kings, would stop by and play a little pool. Once it was said that somebody beat Bojangles out of a thousand dollars at a pool game. Another regular at Dad's was the author Richard Wright. Dad was very selective. As for Richard Wright, we didn't know he was a writer until his book came out—then we were so proud of him. Far as we knew, Mr. Wright worked for the post office. This was the early 1940s. The pool halls were important—we talked a lot about politics. The Washington Park forum was important, with those great radical speakers Claude

Lightfoot and Ishmael Flory. And as it turned out, my early activities made a big difference to my later opportunities.

I found that there were some interesting blemishes on my record. While in the army, I had applied to go to Officer Candidate School, but they said I had been associated with the wrong people. That wasn't race, they said. That was association. For instance, they knew I was a supporter of Ishmael Flory, a Red. They had tracked me all the way back to grammar school, looking for subversive connections. And I had been tracked by the infamous Chicago "Red Squad." I had been a member of the Youth Council of the WPA, the Works Progress Administration. We got paid to work on various public projects—I was there in 1940 when Eleanor Roosevelt opened the South Side Community Art Center, now the oldest such WPA establishment still going. Many of the participants were pretty radical. My big brother, Walter, was in that too. It hurt my mama's feelings that the other boys were going to Officer Candidate School, but I was not. Welton Taylor, one of the first black professors in the medical school at the University of Illinois at Chicago, had been a Tuskegee airman. His mother and my mother were like sisters. His uncle was the great musician and composer W. C. Handy, and their family was almost like aristocracy. How could my mama brag to them, when I did not go to Officer Candidate School?

Years later, I requested and got at least part of my FBI files from the 1940s onward. It became pretty obvious that if I'd kept my mouth shut I would have been an officer in the army. Later I would have at least been a principal in the Chicago Public Schools system. I finished my master's at the University of Chicago in 1954, and I had more academic training than any other black in the system. I was very much in demand. Yet it happened more than once, during job searches, that they would choose someone else and even send them to school. I was on a certain track, because of the FBI and the Red Squad. Without meaning to, they helped me become a career activist.

I was lucky. I got some breaks. After returning from war, from 1946 to about 1950, I was organizing and preparing the movement and continuing my education. I had a wife and young children to support, so I worked in the post office too, while going to college. At Roosevelt University, I got to study with the great John Gibbs St. Clair Drake, who had very recently graduated from the University of Chicago and had coauthored, with Horace Cayton, the book *Black Metropolis: A Study of Negro Life in a Northern City.* That book was a landmark, the first big history of Bronzeville, my Sacred Ground. This is not to take away from earlier efforts, like those of Frederick Hammurabi Robb (I belong to a history club named in his honor) or others. St. Clair Drake was one of the first blacks on the faculty at Roosevelt, and he started one of the first African American studies programs there. He later went to Stanford and started such a program there. He showed me and many others what black history could be.

And it was thanks to St. Clair Drake that I ended up going to graduate school at the University of Chicago, studying with brilliant people like Allison Davis, the anthropologist, and much later becoming friendly with John Hope Franklin. He was not there when I was a student, but he was a big influence later. I will say more about the University of Chicago later on. It was not always the best of places. When I first arrived, I went to the registrar's office to take care of some business, and the woman behind the counter looked at me and said, "Are you sure you are in the right place?" She was obviously wondering what this young black man was doing there. After my first quarter, when I did very well, I took my grade report back to show her—"Yes," I said, "I think I am in the right place."

Allison Davis, who became the first tenured black faculty member—Dr. Julian Herman Lewis was the first black faculty member, back in 1917, but he was not tenured—could not live on campus or in Hyde Park, it was so segregated. He lived over in Woodlawn, and there is now a little space dedicated to him on the west end of the Midway where he used to walk to campus every day. He was the first full tenured black faculty member at a white university. He was St. Clair Drake's mentor, and his work on race and intelligence led to the creation of the Head Start program.

So the University of Chicago was itself part of the conundrum, sometimes progressive, but often not. In 1942, when Allison Davis first joined the faculty, he couldn't even get a haircut in the barbershop in the Reynolds Club, or go to the faculty club, the Quadrangle Club. But that same year, CORE staged a protest there, arranging for Bayard Rustin to go there to try to get a haircut, knowing that he would be passed over for the white customer who came next. That customer was, by design, CORE's Jim Robinson, so the protest began, and eventually the university had to open up the barbershop and the faculty club to blacks. But the university had supported restrictive covenants, even under the leadership of the liberal Robert Maynard Hutchins, and its urban renewal policies in the fifties and sixties would also poison its relationship to our South Side communities.

But there were many very progressive people in and around the university, including the congregation at what would become my church, the First Unitarian Church of Chicago. It dates back to 1836, though it only moved into the Hyde Park location at Fifty-Seventh and Woodlawn in 1897. It was a Unitarian Universalist church that welcomed people with all different beliefs. I started going there around 1954, after my daughter, Ermetra, turned to me one day and asked, "Daddy, where is God?" I had always gone to church with my parents, but I was pretty skeptical about religious beliefs. But now I thought to myself that I did not have the right to impose my skeptical beliefs on my daughter. So we joined the Unitarian Universalists. I felt comfortable there and knew my children would be exposed to many different views there. Ermetra became one of the first members of the now famous Chicago Children's Choir, which started there and was itself part of the civil rights movement, aiming to bring different people together through song. And it was practically on the campus of the university.

I did not leave the university because of the racial pressure. Throughout my time there, there was a strong sense that something big was going to happen. I moved into teaching in the early 1950s, and one night, I happened to see Dr. King on TV—this was in about December of 1955—with Mrs. Parks and E. D. Nixon. They were talking about the Montgomery bus boycott. I immediately flew to Montgomery and became immersed in the movement. By that time I had completed everything for my doctorate except the dissertation, the paper. Allison Davis used to call me every week, asking, "When are you gonna finish that paper?" He was still the first black scholar to receive a Ph.D. and join the faculty at the University of Chicago, and he wanted me to finish. That was not as important to me.

In Alabama, I encountered Mr. A. Philip Randolph, who was also part of the leadership of the Progressive Party and in many ways the dean of the civil rights movement, and Dr. W. E. B. Du Bois, the brilliant intellectual. The power of these intellectual giants was magnetic. While still in graduate school, I had been teaching in a high school out in Gary, Indiana, but when I saw Dr. King, I simply took off, hopping on a plane to Montgomery that weekend. In Montgomery, Dr. King's church was packed to the rafters. Before Dr. King spoke, another person—a very tough guy—spoke to the crowd: "If they strike me," he said, "I'm going to strike them back." I never saw him speak again. He was a pastor, but they got rid of him, and Dr. King became the head of that church.

Dr. Martin Luther King Jr.

So I was watching TV that night, and I saw this good-looking young man who spoke the way I felt. At that time Martin was just twenty-six years old. I heard that sermon with the theme "I'm Tired." And that was it for me. I jumped on a plane and flew down to Montgomery. I was so enthralled that I wanted to be a part of it. And as early as 1956, I helped arrange for him to visit Chicago. I had joined Hyde Park's First Unitarian Church, and some of us invited Dr. King to speak there. But King was already so popular that we had to move the event to nearby Rockefeller Memorial Chapel on the University of Chicago campus, though even that was not big enough for the crowds that came to hear Dr. King.

Then, only a few years later, Rev. Fred Shuttlesworth, the pastor of Bethel Baptist Church in Birmingham, came up to Chicago to talk about Birmingham. He spoke at the Bethesda Baptist Church at Fifty-Third and Michigan Avenue. He was so eloquent and so impassioned in describing the situation in Birmingham and its problems and all. It was Fred Shuttlesworth, a true, forceful activist, who first pushed Dr. Martin Luther King Jr. to come over and help lead the movement in Birmingham, and he also helped cofound the Southern Christian Leadership Conference in 1957. His house had been bombed in 1956, and he would say that he was blown into history. Through it all, he stayed committed to nonviolence. I had been following that movement, the events leading up to the Birmingham campaign of 1963, as often as I could, both because of my roots there and because of my instinct that this was going to assume national significance.

In the company of Fred Shuttlesworth, I went on several ventures and marches in the South, in the course of which Dr. King got to know me, as did others. And Shuttlesworth's early visit to Chicago inspired all sorts of action. For one, when Shuttlesworth came up to Bethesda Baptist, Jim Forman was also there. Jim, who had also graduated from Roosevelt, was teaching at what is now Kenwood Academy High School. He got so fired up that he decided to head down to North Carolina, where along with Ella Jo Baker he started what eventually became the Student Nonviolent Coordinating Committee (SNCC).

When I first got down to Birmingham I called up my cousins in the old neighborhood. Some of them still resided in the family house that had belonged to my grandparents. My cousin's reaction was somewhat startling initially. I said, "I'm down here to see Martin King," and my cousin said, "Well, don't come by here." He didn't need the trouble. He knew that police commissioner Bull Connor had his eye on the community.

My Birmingham relatives, my daddy's people, were "good livers." They had longevity but they were not rash. My daddy went down there to attend a family funeral. The police approached Daddy on the street, and he made some sort of belligerent remark to the cop. My Birmingham cousins had to say to the cop, "Can't you see he's crazy?" They were afraid he'd get himself into a fight, and they didn't need that kind of trouble.

My relatives in Birmingham were serious, hardworking, educated people. Their children were prepared. When the breakthrough came they were the beneficiaries of the changes. Their children became officials, administrators, lawyers, and leaders. The family knew the other old-line black families of Birmingham. Alma Powell, the wife of General Colin Powell, came from Birmingham, from the same social circle. Her family supported Dr. King. They were friendly as well with the family of Condoleezza Rice, whose father was a prominent black pastor in Birmingham, although the Rice family was not openly active in support of Dr. King and the movement.

I became acquainted with Dr. King, and he referred to me as Brother Black. I found him fascinating. I was older, and he treated me as an older brother; his attitude was respectful, and I felt kinship and honor. Dr. King sensed that he needed us elders and the many who, like me, had our heritage in the South, our families having fled the South, and who had experienced the segregated army. He knew we were ready. And I needed the leadership. I was an activist, but I needed the leadership of a figure like Dr. King. People felt they knew about him, but they didn't know him. It took some time before his historic vision and his historic importance became really clear, really timeless.

I commuted between Alabama and Chicago over those years, helping to build a network of support for Dr. King's movement. Sometimes he called me "TD" instead of Brother Black, and I called him "Doc."

His charisma was undeniable. Anyway, I was there with him when we had those Birmingham marches organized by Fred Shuttlesworth. Shuttlesworth had moved to Cincinnati in 1961 but stayed very involved in the campaign in Birmingham, where he was convicted of parading without a permit. That was in 1963, and the case eventually made it to the Supreme Court, in *Shuttlesworth v. Birmingham* in 1969, when his conviction was overturned. I was there in the spring of 1963, at the 16th Street Baptist Church, the site later that year of the bombings that killed those four young girls, and the site where James Bevel organized the children's marches. I remember walking out of that church in the May protest marches, and Doc dropped to his knees and said, "Can we pray?" The mob and the police began to beat the people. Bull Connor had them attack us with dogs and fire hoses. The whole world saw it. It became an international event because of the attacks on the protestors. But when I walked out of the 16th Street Baptist Church and confronted that violence, I knew in my heart at that moment, I knew that I was not profoundly nonviolent. For me, nonviolence was a tactic. But it was an important tactic, and my admiration for Dr. King made me adopt it. But I could not share it at the spiritual level of Dr. King.

But other aspects of Dr. King's philosophy were more deeply rooted in me. Now, to back up a bit, in 1959 or 1960, Mr. A. Philip Randolph had challenged the president of the American Federation of Labor and Congress of Industrial Organizations (the AFL-CIO) about segregation in the unions, pointing out how in the railroad industry few blacks became skilled craftsmen. Randolph was a legendary figure who had founded the Brotherhood of Sleeping Car Porters back in the twenties, when it was the first predominantly black labor union, and it was the only all-black union to become part of the AFL-CIO. He had a great record as a labor leader, including serving on the executive council of the AFL-CIO. He was a major figure in trying to get the unions to support the civil rights movement. Responding to Mr. Randolph's challenge from the convention floor, AFL-CIO president George Meany said, "And who the hell chose you to be the spokesman for the Negro people?" This insult propelled us to organize the Negro American Labor Council (NALC), which supported the civil rights movement from within the labor movement. I became the local president of the NALC and continued my career as a labor organizer (I was very involved with the Chicago Teachers Union).

We began to organize all over the country. We had a national convention in a suburb of New York City in 1961. Dr. King attended that conference, and there he enunciated his feelings publicly for the first time about the Vietnam War. The young blacks and Latinos were volunteering for that war not out of patriotism but because of poverty. But we needed to consolidate our movement. We needed a focal event to bring it together.

Meany, trying to patch things up, had invited Dr. King to address the AFL-CIO convention in 1961, and King used that opportunity to criticize the union for censuring Randolph, which they had done that year. He called for help from the NALC, and talked about how the unions needed to be part of the civil rights movement, pointing out their common causes and tactics. He saw very clearly the links between jobs and justice. He was a democratic socialist from early on in his career, and my labor organizing was very much in his spirit in that way.

Then in January of 1963, at the national board meeting of the NALC, Mr. Randolph announced, "I will declare a march on Washington." We looked around at each other and thought, "How in the world is he going to do that?" But he did know what he was doing. He wanted results. Back in 1941, Randolph threatened to call a national march on Washington to press for the Fair Employment Practices Act, but President Roosevelt did not want that march to happen. To preempt it, he issued Executive Order 8802, which banned and prohibited segregation in the defense industries and military resources. Now it's two decades later, and Mr. Randolph comes up with this idea again. He didn't have to pull it off in 1941. But this time he did, and we did. Randolph later asked King to take the nominal leadership of the March on Washington, because by then Birmingham had become such an international symbol. It was the passing of the torch.

After Mr. Randolph asked Dr. King to take over the leadership of the March on Washington for Jobs and Freedom—it would take place in August of 1963—some of the more conservative leaders of the movement were reluctant. The NAACP were reluctant; they didn't think it would work.

But Randolph used King as an organizing factor, a public figure and symbol. The actual logistical and political organizing was led by Bayard Rustin. Rustin was a pacifist and a leading organizer of the movement, with vast experience extending back to the organizing of the Pullman porters. He was a protégé of Randolph's. He had, before 1941, been a member of the Communist Party, and he was gay. He helped with the founding of CORE, and he traveled to India in 1948 to learn about Gandhian nonviolence. In the fifties, Rustin and E. D. Nixon, a fellow porter who later became a leader of the freedom movement in Alabama, were helping organize the Montgomery bus boycott. These were historic, deep ties that helped pull the disparate forces together.

Back in Chicago, we now had organized groups representing all the major civil rights organizations: SNCC, CORE, and the NALC all had chapters. We had already begun to form a coalition, with the goal of coordinating our local efforts and getting people to Washington for the march. So we expanded the CCCO—the Coordinating Council of Community Organizations, or the Triple-C O—which had been started in 1962 and would later be under the leadership of Al Raby. There was plenty of politicking taking place. The Chicago Urban League had years ago fired its executive director, Sidney Williams, who was too much an activist for the Urban League's funders. They were uncomfortable with the militancy of CORE and later of SNCC, and with the nationalism and African identity of the Muslims. I had first met Sidney in London at an international gathering with Cheddi Jagan, the nationalist statesman from Guyana. Joe Jefferson, my old mentor from the South Side Wabash YMCA, was there too. When he returned to the States, Joe organized the high school youth councils and elementary school youth councils in the Black Belt area of the city, as he had organized the Negro Labor Relations League (NLRL) years before.

As the March on Washington began to get organized, it became apparent that there were tensions between Dr. King and the leadership of the NAACP and the Urban League, the old-line civil rights organizations. They were somewhat envious because Dr. King had usurped what they imagined to be their role on a national level. They had the major resources to support the event, but Dr. King could be more independent. The only organizations that had more resources and a bigger role were the labor unions. This became apparent with the election of Lyndon Baines Johnson in 1964. The United Auto Workers financed the March on Washington to a major degree. This was because of the reluctance of the NAACP and the Urban League—they were afraid to be identified with the march, because they doubted it would be a success.

At any rate, Dr. King asked Bayard Rustin to call me and Larry Landry here in Chicago to take over the co-chairmanship of the Midwest mobilization for the march. We didn't remain involved in the in-fighting about this at the national level. We returned to Chicago, and we were given work space at the union hall of the United Packinghouse Workers. We held many rallies there. We had a crew of experienced organizers. Among them was a young Jewish fellow, Sam Ackerman, who mobilized a lot of the whites. We began the logistical arrangements, booking charter buses and even entire railroad trains. It was not diffi-cult work—people knew about and supported the goals of the march. We were overwhelmed with requests to participate. Young people from CORE and SNCC threw themselves into the campaign. Soon even the NAACP came back and wanted to be included. In Chicago, too, there was friction and competition between the traditional civil rights organi-zations. The then leader of the Urban League, Bill Berry, didn't want to stain his reputation by associating with militants. But when it became clear that we were a force to be reckoned with, then every organization wanted to claim credit for the march.

Sidney Williams had been the leader of the Chicago Urban League. He was an aggressive progressive, fighting for the integration of schools, jobs, and public accommodations. But in the mid-1950s, there was pres-sure to hire someone more moderate. That's when they brought in Bill Berry from the West. He was a savvy fundraiser and was able to attract major white donors. These same donors would not talk to me, but they would talk to Bill. The Chicago Urban League under Berry's leadership became one of the most well-funded Urban Leagues in the country. And he did, eventually, help fund the Chicago contingent of thousands of people to the March on Washington.

But there was always a certain fear of radicalism, of being red-baited, of having the civil rights movement discredited. There was a skittish-ness and avoidance in some quarters. Some organizations had radicals in leadership, who were fired despite being brilliant strategists. The organizations were too afraid, so they tended to employ more moderate managers.

Larry Landry wanted to be a part of it, but the organizing in Chicago became my responsibility. Very quickly, Charlie Hayes got involved; he was a great friend who had helped organize the United Packinghouse Workers of America and form the Coalition of Black Trade Unionists (CBTU), and he went on to win Harold Washington's seat from the First Congressional District, after Harold became mayor. We began to get requests to be a part of the Chicago contingent by the hundreds, even thousands. At this time, I was teaching at Hyde Park Academy High School, but I still had time to organize. The dedication of the young people was fantastic. The office was staffed twenty-four hours a day with volunteers from the movement. So all I had to do was go there and check in. On the trains we had about three thousand, and with the people who went by their own means, we ended up with more than four thousand from Chicago for the March on Washington. We filled up several trains; in fact, they were overloaded. We had musicians on the trains entertaining and leading sing-alongs. We had Studs Terkel working the aisles with his tape recorder, interviewing riders. "What brings you to the March on Washington?" he would ask everyone, old people and tiny kids. And he played their responses on his radio program.

The Pullman porters organized and arranged for the trains, but the attitudes of pedestrians were very hostile, and we were worried. But when we got out to the Mall and saw all the people, it was one of the greatest experiences of my life, of everyone's life. And then when Dr. King gave that speech, the famous "I Have a Dream" speech, the place was awash in tears.

I think of that day when I think of former president Barack Obama. I hope he understands that he is the beneficiary of the hopes and dreams of all kinds of Americans carried forward by those of my generation, struggling to achieve the impossible, but so often doubting that they can do it. His successor, I am sad to say, is contributing to the doubt, not the dream.

Dr. King in Chicago—A Bloody Day

I have never ceased to find Dr. King fascinating. And after 1963, I kept working to pave the way for his entry into Chicago. I worked closely with Charlie Hayes, who later became a member of Congress. We raised money to fund Dr. King's work in Chicago. And we still focused on economic justice. Even after Executive Order 8802, which made discrimination in the war industry illegal and helped a lot of the well-trained black workers who were stuck sweeping floors to move up into better positions, economic justice was far off. In Chicago, they had built the Altgeld Gardens housing project, and in Detroit the Brewster Homes, specifically to house the influx of workers for the defense industries in the build-up to war. But because of discrimination these housing units were built to be separate; there were white projects and black projects. And they stayed separate. These, as I will explain later, became an important focus of some community organizing. Jobs and housing were always issues. Economic justice had to be part of the movement.

When Dr. King came to town for his big campaign in the Chicago area, in January of 1966, he focused on open housing, an end to housing segregation. This discrimination, the redlining and so on, has been described in powerful detail by my old DuSable friend Dempsey Travis, in his book *An Autobiography of Black Chicago*. Dr. King was, we thought, encouraged in this effort by then president Lyndon Johnson. Dr. King moved into slum housing at 1550 South Hamlin, in North Lawndale, though the owners did a quick fixing-up job when they heard he was coming. He felt that to be an effective spokesperson for ending slums he had to better understand the living situation in such areas.

Many dedicated activists had been preparing for this move, the move to bring the civil rights movement north and expand its aims. James Bevel, Bernard LaFayette Jr., Addie Wyatt, Al Raby, Jesse Jackson—they were all working on this. Some wanted Dr. King to target another northern city, but most thought it had to be Chicago: if the movement could win there, it could win anywhere. And Dr. King was able to use places like the Warren Avenue Congregational Church, on the West Side, and Liberty Baptist Church, on the South Side, as organizing headquarters. He opened a headquarters office at Liberty Baptist Church at Forty-Ninth and South Park Boulevard (now known as King Drive). The pastor there was one of King's friends from Morehouse College, Rev. A. P. Jackson—Abraham Patterson Jackson. His father had been friends with King's father, and that was why their two sons ended up together at Morehouse, one of the most important of the historically black colleges. A. P. is one of those featured in the first volume of my *Bridges of Memory*.

But most of the black clergymen were not on King's side. Many did not like his organization, the Southern Christian Leadership Conference (SCLC). Rev. Joseph Jackson, from Olivet Baptist Church in Bronzeville, was for many years the head of the National Baptist Convention (NBC), and he was one of King's enemies. King and his allies had split away from the NBC to form the Progressive National Baptist Convention. Jackson hated King so much that even after King's death, when South Park Boulevard was changed to King Drive, he changed the entrance to his church, so he would not have to have King Drive as his address.

In the summer of 1966, the fight to desegregate housing in the Chicago area had really intensified. In July there was a big rally at Soldier Field, and Dr. King led thousands of marchers to city hall, where he taped our demands to the door. It was hot. All summer it was really hot, and young people were opening the fire hydrants because they did not have access to public pools or air conditioning. That was part of what caused the riots, especially in North Lawndale, where King was living. He would go out and talk to everybody. He got a lot of the gang leaders organized. Many of them were willing to give nonviolence a try. But it was a violent summer.

I had written King a letter warning about the danger he faced in coming to Chicago to try to break housing segregation. I had met with organizers several times up at St. Thomas Episcopal Church on Twenty-Sixth and Michigan. We met to organize people advising Dr. King not to come to Chicago. It was too dangerous. There were many people who supported him in their public statements but didn't want him to come to Chicago—such as those black aldermen who would prefer not to push. They were known as the "Silent Six," Claude Holman and the rest. They had us come to a meeting with these alderman, and they talked about Dr. King like he was a dog, nothing but a troublemaker. After that meeting, when it became clear that they would even try to undermine him in the black community, and that police protection could not be relied upon, I took it upon myself to write a letter to Dr. King. In my letter, I asked him not to come to Chicago, warning him that he would run into danger.

Interestingly, Dr. King still believed he would be protected. It was the same way in Selma; he thought the middle class in Selma would be the ones to support him. But they weren't. The truth is, Dr. King's reliable base was ordinary poor people—those who had the least to lose and the most to gain from the struggle. Much of the income in the black community was tied to the system, to the Daley machine.

But Mayor Daley was at least determined that King would not be martyred in Chicago, so police were assigned to protect him and the marchers. My old friend Rudy Nimocks, whose mother used to play piano at the Grand Terrace Ballroom, was one of those assigned to protect the marchers.

But there were lots of protest marches that summer, in 1966. These were big protests. On the Southwest Side, by Gage Park and Marquette Park, we picketed the real estate agents who were guilty of redlining and all sorts of discrimination. Restrictive covenants may have been ruled unenforceable by the Supreme Court, but Chicago was still a very segregated place. The laws prohibiting discrimination in housing were not enforced. The slumlords were as bad as ever. The Chicago Freedom Movement, Dr. King's movement in Chicago, called for the end of slums, and also for equal educational opportunities.

The protests were met with incredible hostility from the whites, who screamed and shouted every kind of obscenity at us and were always throwing things at us. It was not like the South, where the police attacked us. Here the police tried to protect us, but the mobs were worse than ever. Then, at the big march in Marquette Park, on August 5, someone threw a rock that hit Dr. King on the head so he sank to his knees. I thought to myself, "If one of those . . . MFers hits me like that, the nonviolent movement is over." I could practice nonviolence in the South, but not in the North. I could not put up with any shit here. Dr. King said later that he had never witnessed such hate-filled and hostile mobs as he had in Chicago. But his faith in nonviolence never failed him. Father Pfleger, the great activist priest of St. Sabina down in Auburn Gresham, who has done so much to try to end gun violence, was inspired to become a priest by what he saw in Marquette Park when he was a young man, by how Dr. King had the strength to love in the face of all that hatred. He tells people that he became a priest because of Dr. King.

The police, his supporters, and the gang leaders had all tried to protect Dr. King, but the situation was dangerous, and he was getting criticized from all over. The segregationists rallied and rioted against us. We had all received nonviolence training, but it was quite challenging not to pick up a brick and fight back. Young people in the Black Power movement, like Monroe Sharp, challenged Dr. King at Liberty Baptist Church later that August. They claimed that nonviolence had failed, that more aggressive tactics were needed now. The radical young people began to jump on him right away. Even Jim Forman worried that SNCC might not stick to nonviolence.

And a big confrontation arose over the plan to march for open housing in the white suburb of Cicero. That was even more dangerous than Marquette Park. When a march was called in the suburb of Cicero, we felt that Dr. King would be in severe danger. There were violent groups threatening his life if he showed up. There was no reason to believe he would receive adequate police protection. Even Daley was worried and desperately wanted him to call it off. And someone persuaded King not to go. There was a "summit agreement," with Daley agreeing to enforce the fair housing laws, and King called this a victory, though he probably knew in his heart that Daley would not follow up. Anyway, he did agree not to march in Cicero, though some of his supporters insisted on going there, especially Bob Lucas and people from CORE. They were met with plenty of violence, but it would have been worse if Dr. King had gone.

Plantation Politics

Understand that my views of Chicago politics—what I would come to call "plantation politics"—were at that time pretty complicated. My involvement was wider than I have indicated, which is why I came to be trusted by Dr. King. In 1955, Emmett Till's funeral in Chicago had caused big protests over his brutal murder. I participated in those, and a few years later, I helped organize the Chicago League of Negro Voters to challenge the Daley machine's control over the "Negro vote." This became the "March on Conventions Movement for Freedom Now," run in Chicago by me and Bennett Johnson, a fellow teacher at Farragut High School, but part of a national movement led by Randolph and King. We led mass marches to the site of the 1960 Republican convention.

In 1963 I ran for alderman, as part of a coalition of independent black candidates. We wanted to challenge the "Silent Six," the black aldermen who were controlled by Daley with the help of William "Big Bill" Dawson—Daley robbed him of his political power—and later Ralph Metcalfe, though Ralph was in many ways a sympathetic figure who quietly tried to support me when possible. And that same year we organized a huge protest against Chicago Public Schools Superintendent Benjamin Willis. We got over two hundred thousand people to boycott the Chicago Public Schools to protest Willis and his segregationist policies, including the "Willis Wagons" that I mentioned earlier. That was when I called for us to "end plantation politics" in Chicago. I compared some black politicians to the house slaves who did the master's bidding, who were more compromised by the system than the field slaves. I did not win my run for alderman, but my words caught on.

Later in the sixties, I was asked by my friend Abner Mikva, who had decided to run for Congress, to run for the state senate seat from his area to enhance our chance of victory. This would bring out more black voters, which would also help Ab's congressional campaign. President Lyndon Johnson was in trouble—deep trouble. LBJ was wrestling to get control of the U.S. House. He needed all the votes he could get in order to pass his legislative agenda. So the congressional races took on renewed significance. Ab Mikva, a popular local progressive who had served as a state representative, was now running for the Second Congressional District seat. But Dick Newhouse, an African American who was not very well known, decided he was going to run against me for that state senate seat—against Mikva's wishes.

When Mikva decided to run for the House seat, he wanted my help. I was very well known by then. LBJ's main black ally in Congress, Adam Clayton Powell Jr. of New York, was embroiled in a couple of scandals. The progressive editor of the *Chicago Defender* newspaper had been fired, and was now working for Powell. He called me to ask what it would take to get me out of the race. They saw I would bring in the votes and increase Mikva's chances of election. But apparently the president didn't want another person he could not control. LBJ did not want Mikva to win.

So now they had to figure out a way to get me out of there. I had three times as many signatures as I needed to get myself on the ballot. A wealthy radical philanthropist, Lucy Montgomery, was raising money like mad for me. I was very comfortable. I knew I could bring votes in. Larry Landry calls me and says Tim, two black candidates should not be running against each other. He asks me for a meeting so we can talk it over. I'm confident. He said Mikva and the Independent Voters of Illinois Independent Precinct Organization, the IVI-IPO, wanted to meet. They, of course, supported me. But then the leadership of the local Urban League and the CCCO got involved, and they said, "Why don't you guys make an agreement to let us decide which one of you will run?" My friends at IVI-IPO wanted to know why. People were very suspicious of the motives of those who were proposing this meeting, but they were just following the directives of those at the national level.

We met late at night at the Urban League offices in what is now known as the Swift Mansion. There was a lot of double-dealing and backstabbing, and I began to feel naive. I went over with Clarice Durham, an old friend of mine from high school who became a great activist. She worked with the Progressive Party and with Ishmael Flory and was always dedicated to social progress. We had lots of supporters; Newhouse had few. I had professors, judges, all supporting me. But that very evening, after I had signed the agreement they wanted me to sign, one of the parties involved called Newhouse and said don't drop out now. Again, he had gotten his instructions from the national office. Don't drop out now, just wait—that was the advice the leadership of the Urban League and CCCO gave Newhouse. They began to pick off my supporters right after that first meeting, after I signed the paper, despite my having the support of Mikva and the IVI-IPO.

When they started picking off my supporters, I thought wait a minute, we haven't settled this matter yet. They said, "We don't want to get in the middle of a conflict." I asked, "How will we know how you chose the person that you are going to support?" They answered, "Oh, you don't need to know that, that's none of your business." Then one night at 3:00 or 4:00 A.M. they called me to a meeting in half an hour. I went. My young son Tim heard me leaving the house, and asked me, "Dad, where are you going in the middle of the night?" I told him, "Don't worry. Just some business to take care of." When I got there, no one was there but that same leadership from the Urban League and CCCO. They announced they had decided to throw their support behind the candidacy of Newhouse. The janitor, who was outside listening in, said, "Goddam!" They had me agree in good faith to abide by this agreement which was not worth a nickel. I never went into that Urban League building again. To me it was the scene of the double cross.

As things turned out, Newhouse did not bring in the additional votes. But he did exactly what the national party expected of him. Ab Mikva lost in 1966 due to low turnout in the black wards. Eventually, after redistricting in the 1970s, Mikva moved out to Evanston. He would not run against a black candidate, Ralph Metcalfe. Before running for Congress, Mikva had served in the Illinois House representing a district that was predominantly black, but there was no real conflict. Blacks supported him, just as they supported Alderman Leon "Len" Despres. We had the ability then as now to discern genuine progressives. We judged them by their deeds. When Despres was the only alderman in the Chicago City Council to criticize Daley's plantation politics and urban renewal policies, we used to say, "There's only one black man in the city council, and he's white."

I was stunned and a bit disillusioned by this whole experience. I could not believe that the White House would intervene directly in such a local race. As my old friend and supporter Clarice Durham recalls it: "I supported Tim's unsuccessful run as an Independent candidate for alderman of the 4th Ward against the Machine candidate Claude Holman. And I appeared on his behalf before the Board of the Coordinating Council of Community Organizations (CCCO) seeking its endorsement of his run for the office of Illinois State Senator. However, they endorsed Richard Newhouse, believing he had a better chance of winning. Newhouse did win and served in the Senate for several years." But that is not the whole story, as I have indicated.

Ab Mikva went on to become a distinguished federal judge, White House Counsel under President Clinton, and, when teaching at the University of Chicago Law School, a mentor to the young Barack Obama. Like Despres, he was a genuine progressive. We judged them by their deeds, of course, and what they were doin' matched what they were sayin'. I am glad to have worked with them.

It's true 1966 was a very hard year. The miraculous does indeed take a little longer. But Dr. King had brought the civil rights movement to Chicago and expanded it, brought it together with the peace movement and the movement for economic justice. Perhaps the miraculous got a little closer.

Mama (Mattie Hardin McConner Black) and Daddy (Timuel Dixon Black) had their photo taken to send to me while I was serving in the U.S. Army in Europe during World War II, to assure me they were alive and well back home.

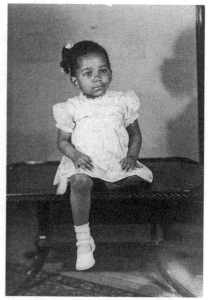

My children, Kerrigan and Ermetra.

My son, Timuel Kerrigan Black, known as Kerrigan,
musicologist and recording artist (1953–1993).

My daughter, Ermetra Black Johnson, poet and writer.

With my wife, Zenobia Johnson Black. We met while campaigning for Harold Washington in 1982.

My big brother, attorney Walter McConner Black (1915–1996).

Harlem Globetrotters team owner Abe Saperstein recruited most of his players from Chicago's Wendell Phillips High School. The 1930–31 team included (*from left*) Abe Saperstein, Toots Wright, Byron Long, Inman Jackson, William Oliver, and (*seated*) Al "Runt" Pullins. Each played against my brother, Walter, on the Tilden squad. But Walter went off to college instead of signing with the Globetrotters.

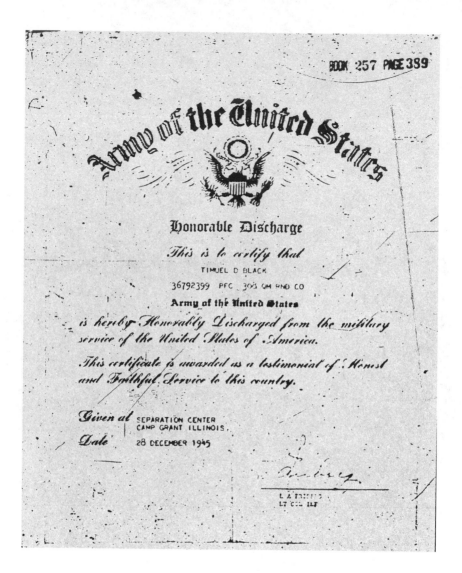

Army of the United States

Honorable Discharge

This is to certify that

TIMUEL D BLACK

36792399 PFC 303 QM RND CO

Army of the United States

is hereby Honorably Discharged from the military service of the United States of America.

This certificate is awarded as a testimonial of Honest and Faithful Service to this country.

Given at SEPARATION CENTER
CAMP GRANT ILLINOIS.

Date 28 DECEMBER 1945

L A TITUS
LT COL ILT

My military discharge papers from 1945. After I was framed and court-martialed, the charges against me were dropped, and I received an honorable discharge, three Overseas Service bars, the European–Middle Eastern Theater Ribbon with four Bronze Battle Stars, a Good Conduct medal, a World War II Victory medal, and the Croix de Guerre with Palm from the government of France.

Here's "Mr. Black" in the 1956 yearbook of Roosevelt
High School in Gary, Indiana, one of my first teaching jobs.
I taught social science and introduced black history.

With Martin Luther King Jr. in the 1960s.

Campaign poster from my run for Fourth Ward alderman in 1963.

COURTESY OF *CHICAGO HISTORY* MAGAZINE.

Celebrating the people's victory with newly elected
Mayor Harold Washington, 1983.

Every year the Mary Herrick Association, named after my revered teacher, awards scholarships to a group of graduating students at my alma mater, DuSable High School.

I deeply enjoy sharing our stories with schoolchildren.
Black History Month is my busiest time of year.

Speaking about oral history at the annual conference of the
American Educational Research Association with Bill Ayers
in Chicago, 2005.

On January 18, 2013, at Chicago's annual Interfaith Breakfast honoring the Reverend Dr. Martin Luther King Jr., the City of Chicago awarded its first-ever Champion of Freedom Award to Professor Timuel D. Black. The event was keynoted by civil rights movement hero Congressman John Lewis.

At the RainbowPUSH Coalition with the Reverend Jesse Jackson
Sr. in 2018, on the annual Legacy of Dr. Martin Luther King Jr. tour,
sponsored by the University of Chicago Civic Knowledge Project
and Alumni Association.

PHOTOGRAPH BY BART SCHULTZ

Zenobia and I receive a surprise greeting from former President Barack Obama at the Obama Foundation in Chicago, August 28, 2018.

{ CHAPTER 4 }

A Life in Teaching

My political life and my life in education, as a student, teacher, and administrator, have been part of the same story, the story of my Sacred Ground. It is no accident that this community has produced such great political figures. There was Oscar De Priest, who was also from Florence, Alabama, and who became the first black alderman in Chicago in 1915 and then from 1929 to 1935 the first black congressman after Reconstruction, representing the First Congressional District, now represented by Bobby Rush. There was Harold Washington, the first black mayor of Chicago, and Carol Moseley Braun, the first black woman to serve in the United States Senate, from 1993 to 1996. There was Jesse Jackson, who was sent to Chicago by Dr. King in the 1960s to run Operation Breadbasket and who went on to found the RainbowPUSH Coalition and become the first serious black presidential candidate, in 1984 and 1988. And then we produced the first black president of the United States, Barack Obama, first elected in 2008. And the first black First Lady, Michelle Obama, from the South Shore neighborhood. This Sacred Ground has made history again and again. And whatever some might say, it is pretty miraculous. There are still a lot of miracles that need to be done, but that does not mean that our history is less than miraculous.

So my education was a very political education, just coming from this Sacred Ground. Tim Black's history is just part of this black history, going back to even before my daddy took me to the Wabash Avenue YMCA sometime in 1926 to hear Carter G. Woodson call for a "Negro History Week." That later became Black History Month. My formal schooling was not always so powerful, but it sometimes was, and when I became a teacher I tried to get that message out—you come from people, you are somebody, trouble don't last forever. That optimism is important, to keep on keepin' on. As my friend of eighty-three years Clarice Durham put it, recalling our time at DuSable, "Even today Tim and I talk about how fortunate we were to have been in a school environment that promoted academic achievement, school pride, and awareness of and involvement in social issues. The inscription, 'Peace If Possible but Justice at Any Rate,' was inscribed on the proscenium above the stage in the school auditorium—a constant reminder of the ideal society we should work to achieve. With that background, it is not surprising that by the time we met again [after high school], we had both become social activists, working for peace and justice worldwide."

And after all of Mama's nagging, and also thanks to the FBI, I did eventually go to college. I started at Roosevelt University in 1949 and graduated in 1952 with a bachelor of arts in sociology (graduating in three years even while working at the Post Office), and then went on to earn my master's degree from the University of Chicago. I could have gone to many different places, but Roosevelt was close to home and had a reputation for inclusiveness. As I explained, it was a political education in itself, and I also had the opportunity to study with St. Clair Drake. He was the one who urged me to go to the University of Chicago for graduate school, where I started out in the School of Social Service Administration before switching to the Social Sciences Division, where I could study with Allison Davis, who supervised my graduate work for that Ph.D. before I went off to follow Dr. King. I told myself then that if that doctorate was not on the horizon by the time I was forty, I would forget about it. It wasn't, and I did. The civil rights movement was more important.

It was while I was at the University of Chicago that I began teaching. I began as a student teacher in 1954, at my old school, DuSable. The great Mary Herrick was my mentor there; she was very active in the Chicago Teachers Union and taught me a lot about how to make that union a real union. And about how to teach—she supervised my student teaching. After I returned to DuSable after teaching in Gary for a year, she was going off to do union work for a couple of years and requested that I teach her classes. I owe my teaching career to her. Because of my tainted past and associations with radicals, I would never have gotten my teaching certificate if she had not mobilized support for me. The Chicago Board of Education was very racist in its certification procedures, and they used racist tactics that were a lot like those used in the South to deny blacks the vote, such as rigged oral exams. I would never have been certified if Mary Herrick had not used her influence on the board to get them to approve my certification, which of course meant that I would be paid more and could get tenure and a more secure position.

Miss Herrick was a graduate of the University of Chicago and white. She was a great teacher and also a brilliant researcher who later published an important book, *The Chicago Schools: A Social and Political History*. Her students all loved her, and when Harold Washington was elected mayor, he worked with a number of us from DuSable to declare a Mary J. Herrick day in Chicago. She was an academic and an activist, a labor leader and a great teacher. I was so fortunate to be her student. It is characteristic that she was the one who had arranged for the great leftist reformer and economist, and later U.S. Senator, Paul Douglas to be our DuSable commencement speaker. And I still recall going over to her house by the University of Chicago with John Johnson and other DuSable students—she welcomed her students to her home

After my student teaching at DuSable, I went to teach at Roosevelt High School in Gary, Indiana. But Mary Herrick always wanted me to come back to DuSable, which I soon did, until around 1958 or so, when I was called to go over to the West Side, to Farragut High School, because they were having some racial conflicts, and a young black student had been killed. I had also considered Park Manor High School. The principal there asked me, "Do you know how to treat Negro students?" and I replied, "Just like everyone else." I went to Farragut. Bennett Johnson was also working at Farragut, and at one point the superintendent of schools told the principal there to get rid of Johnson and Black. But the students there, both black and white, heard about this and protested, shouting, "What you doin' to Mr. Black?" Many of the students there were from immigrant families, and some of them went on to become active in SNCC and the civil rights movement.

The school system did not like the way we were teaching at Farragut. We were bringing in a lot of black history and talking about the civil rights movement, talking about the lunch counter sit-ins going on in the South. When we invited one of the sit-in leaders to Farragut, Chicago Public Schools (CPS) wanted to fire us. Bennett did get fired. He was an old friend from Roosevelt, another friend of Harold's from those days, and had organized protests to get black clerks hired on State Street. In 1966 he helped arrange the meeting between Dr. King and Elijah Muhammad, the leader of the Nation of Islam. He became a publishing executive and the founder of Path Press.

Bennett and I both saw the civil rights movement as including the fight against racism in the job market and unions, including the teachers union. This involvement in organizing teachers was what paved the path to my role in NALC, the Negro American Labor Council. Because I was a teachers union activist, I was elected president of the Chicago chapter and stayed there for a long time as the organization grew. We soon had about a thousand blacks in the organization, and we were very active. We organized against things like the racial exclusion in the skilled trades apprenticeship programs at the Chicago Board of Education's Washburne Trade School. The board tried to ignore the evidence we had proving racial discrimination there. So we got Adam Clayton Powell Jr. to block federal funds to Washburne, and that made Daley go to the White House to get the funds. We continued to try to integrate Washburne, but as it desegregated, the unions began to pull out and it had a hard time. The Culinary School eventually moved to Kennedy-King, one of the City Colleges.

I have indicated my political opposition to Mayor Daley and the "Silent Six," the black aldermen he controlled. Daley, and the superintendent of schools, Benjamin Willis, were always trying to deny that there was segregation in Chicago. When I would demand that we "end plantation politics," Daley and his cronies would say, "There are no ghettos in Chicago," or "There is no segregation in Chicago." But the segregation was there for the whole world to see, and after we challenged Daley and the school system in 1963, it got a lot harder for them to say things like that. He got booed off the stage one time, in Grant Park. After that incident, I heard from the Mayor's people that he wanted to see me. I said "OK, we will be there." They said that he just wanted to see me, alone. But I knew better than to let him use me, or get me in there without someone to back up my account of what went on. I declined the invitation.

I thought, and still think, that our opposition to the first Mayor Daley was very significant. One time, one of our independents, Charlie

Chew—"a vote for Chew is a vote for you"—actually won, in the Seventeenth Ward. And for my part, I wanted to show my students that a black person could run as an independent and not get killed. I had been in the War, and worked with MLK, and one thing I learned was that you cannot be afraid of the opposition, you cannot let yourself get trapped in fear psychologically. Change comes on the basis of trust, honesty, and authenticity. You need to be able to look at yourself in the mirror. And I always knew how proud Mama and Daddy would be of their children for their courage.

I am also very proud of my work leading the Chicago chapter of the American Federation of Teachers, a national organization that was founded in Chicago in the early twentieth century and that, with the Pullman porters, was fighting segregation from those early years. By the early fifties, the AFT was refusing to charter segregated local chapters, and it even filed a friend-of-the-court brief in *Brown v. the Board of Education.* The AFT strongly supported the March on Washington. My involvement with them has been essential to my work as a labor and civil rights activist. As Dr. King knew, the two cannot be kept apart. I never thought of my work with Dr. King as separate from my work as a labor organizer, despite the racism and segregation of many of the unions. We had been fighting those problems ever since the first Great Migration. I think Mary Herrick, who really made the Chicago Teachers Union a serious union and was vice president of the American Federation of Teachers, saw it that way too. We honored her with a tribute in 1964, but in her characteristic way she wanted to see some practical good come out of it, so we created the Mary J. Herrick Scholarship Fund for DuSable Students. Many years later, I was also honored in this way. I am an activist and organizer, but I am an educator activist and organizer.

There were some sad times during these years, in the late fifties and early sixties, for me personally. My parents had gone on living at 6230 South Vernon, and had been married for over sixty years when my mama died. They had married in 1903. She was diabetic and pretty sickly toward the end, and worried about being a burden on my daddy. But when she was dying, my daddy cried, "Mattie, Mattie, why you leavin' me like this?" After that, he moved in with my brother in South Shore, but he was always saying, "What do I need to be here for? You're doin' all right, and Mattie is gone." He died four or five years later, when he was in his eighties. I still go off sometimes, especially when I am feeling troubled, to talk aloud to them, just the way they talked to their ancestors—my family always carried on that African spiritual tradition of talking to the ancestors. The elders and the ancestors—their voices always matter, if one can learn to listen.

Anyway, by the early sixties many of my friends were urging me to come back to the South Side to teach at Hyde Park Academy High School, so I did. Once again I was one of the few black teachers at the school and dealing with an administration that was treating the black students badly. Now at this time, Hyde Park High had a lot of young students whose parents came up in the second Great Migration around the time of the Second World War and in the 1950s. They were not urban and educated like many of those of us who came up in the first Great Migration. We left, but they were forced off the land and were mostly poor and illiterate, like many of the black soldiers I had served with in the war. They were rural folk, and their children did not enjoy many of the advantages that we did. There was class tension. Many people in my generation did not treat these newcomers very well, to our shame. They were another part of that immigrant story, that universal immigrant story, moving on to seek a better life.

At Hyde Park High, these children of the second Great Migration were dismissed as troublemakers, as undesirables. In Woodlawn and Hyde Park these young people and their families were rejected by the middle-class families, both white and black. The children were discriminated against at school, with the white students on one track and the black students on another. It was a pretty snobbish school, with lots of children from the professors at the University of Chicago. And if you graduated in the top of your class you could go to any college or university in the country. Tracking was how they kept the white parents satisfied.

Of course, I was a troublemaker too. And I could handle them. They respected me because I believed in them. I was like their daddy or grand-daddy. Jeff Fort, who founded the Blackstone Rangers with others too, like Bull Hairston, was one of my students there, and I could handle him, though none of the white teachers could. He could not read well, but he could read, and he had a kind of charisma that you could see even then. He had leadership qualities, intangible leadership qualities. He was a natural leader. And he knew what was going on. I would ask him if he wanted to stay in school, and he would say, "Yeah, Mr. Black, but they are always pickin' on us." He was a tough guy, but exceptional in many ways, and he knew how to listen to people and how people needed respect. He knew how to resolve disputes, and if I had had him there in school with me until he graduated, he could have gone on to achieve prominence in another way. He would have been a leader going to some college or university.

But anyway, in the early 1960s I had to go to Washington for a civil rights meeting, and while I was gone the school put out all these young men, Jeff Fort and his friends. I wanted to get them back, so I went around to the pool hall on Sixty-Third Street near Blackstone where they hung out and said, "Why don't you guys come back to school?" And they said, "Oh, Mr. Black, they don't want us there." I tried to say "No, no, I want you to come back," but they said, "They don't want us there. And we're gonna take it all over." And that's when the Blackstone Rangers—they had already been formed—began that strong gang activity and took over the whole community. They later became the Almighty Black P. Stone Nation, but this was the real beginning of their gang activity. And they later worked with Reverend Fry at First Presbyterian Church in Woodlawn and got funds from the Office of Economic Opportunity to help gang members learn job skills. Jeff Fort was even invited to Richard Nixon's inaugural ball in 1969. But by the seventies, he started getting convicted and going to prison. He is in prison for the rest of his life now, in Colorado. His daughter Ameena Matthews became one of the Peace-keepers, a violence interrupter here on the South Side.

People still wonder about the role of the University of Chicago in this, how they might have wanted the gangs to help clear the area so the university could move in.

Looking back on it, I wish that I could have done more for those students and their families. My generation should have done more to welcome those later arrivals from the South. We were the jazz genera-tion; they were the Delta blues, becoming the electric blues with people like Muddy Waters. As in the army, there was class conflict, class conflict that became cultural conflict.

Jeff Fort could have been like some of those other students, the ones that I mentioned earlier. I think so often of that student Bill Daniels, who graduated from my own alma mater, DuSable High School, in 1956. Again, he was a ward of the state and a foster child, one of those they would classify as "at risk" or "undesirable." In his case too, the admin-istrators and other teachers didn't recognize his other qualities, as a swimmer, chess player, and a good student in many ways, just one who didn't do well on tests. But Bill knew where he wanted to be and got that scholarship to go to college, to Upper Iowa University, where he was the second black student ever and graduated Phi Beta Kappa.

Again, there was the brilliant young Ron Gault, who grew up poor but determined in the next generation after the first Great Migration. He too attended DuSable, and went off to college, becoming an international development banker and marrying the journalist and civil rights leader Charlayne Hunter-Gault. He was another leader.

I have had so many, many wonderful students over the years and it seems that I meet up with someone wherever I go. I have been in England and other parts of Europe when suddenly an old student will recognize me and come up to say, "Hello, Mr. Black, do you remember me from . . ." And I remember a lot of them. I wish I could remember all of them. Both the ones who succeeded and the ones who were not so fortunate. They are all part of this story.

Those were very busy years, the 1950s and 1960s, and I can't even go into all of the things that I was doing. There were dozens of important organizations, like the Americans for Democratic Action, the Chicago Committee to Defend the Bill of Rights, the Chicago League of Negro Voters, Teachers for Integrated Schools, Teachers for Quality Education, the Hyde Park Community Peace Center, and others, some of which I have already mentioned. I was active in all of them. I was always speaking about or writing reports about the conditions in the Chicago public schools, the discrimination against black students and teachers, especially substitute teachers, who were vulnerable. Having tenure allowed me to be more independent, but many black teachers were not so fortunate. When I ran for alderman it was primarily to oppose the Daley machine's support for continued segregation in the schools and across the city.

A letter from the Hyde Park Community Peace Center, dated June 8, 1962, illustrates some of this work and the people involved:

Dear Mr. Black:

We wish to extend our thanks to you for your favorable response to our request for sponsorship for the exciting new Peace Center. The premises should be ready in the next few weeks and as soon as we know when they will be, we are planning to have a reception for our good friends at the Center, prior to formal opening.

We note, however, that we do not have a confirmation of your acceptance as a member of the Advisory Council and would appreciate having this to complete our files.

Even prior to the opening of the Center, we have planned our first Peace Center activity, namely, that of meeting with the Program Chairman [sic] of some forty to fifty community organizations in order to acquaint them with the services that a Peace Center can render in providing appropriate programs for use in their own organizations. We are enclosing a copy of the invitation sent to these Program Chairmen, for your information.

We would certainly appreciate any ideas, suggestions or comments which you may have in connection with this upcoming meeting and invite you to attend, if you find it convenient. You can rest assured that we will continue to keep you informed.

Many thanks and with kindest personal regards—

Very truly yours,

HYDE PARK COMMUNITY PEACE CENTER
Robert Palter – Joseph E. Engel
Co-Chairmen

Some of the other members of the advisory council included Ruth Adams, Philip Altbach, Dr. Sydney Bild, Kenneth Calkins, Hermene Evans, Ella Jenkins, Prof. Paul B. Johnson, Shirley and Sidney Lens, Phyllis Osborne, the Rev. Ellsworth Smith, and Dr. Quentin D. Young. I did confirm, for the Peace Center and so many other organizations.

In those years, the strategy of containment that I spoke of earlier was still a harsh reality. That was when the school board began adding "temporary" portable classrooms to the school playgrounds in the Black Belt, to keep black children from transferring out of overcrowded elementary schools. Again, those trailers, the ones Rosie Simpson called "Willis Wagons" after Superintendent Benjamin Willis, were a concrete manifestation of racial segregation. They were not good learning environments for children, but that was not their real purpose. We knew it and we protested. In October of 1963, we mobilized over two hundred thousand people, maybe a quarter of a million people, to boycott the Chicago public schools. It was a truly historic protest. There was one in October and another one in February 1964, when almost as many students boycotted the schools. This was not long after the March on Washington, and we were still mobilizing hundreds of thousands of people. These were also "Freedom Marches," with thousands of people marching to CPS headquarters demanding an end to segregation in the schools. As in Birmingham, our actions were broadcast around the world. Superintendent Willis soon had to resign.

Anyway, I was very much in demand, and when the students at Wright Junior College up on the North Side started demanding that the college hire some black administrators and faculty, I was recruited to go there, as a dean, assistant dean of transfer and general studies, with professorial standing. I did not want to give up teaching, so I insisted that I teach at least one course a year. I taught History 110, Afro-American History.

I was recruited by Wright partly because I had already started doing a lot of educational administration. I quit CPS in 1966 to work as assistant director of the United States Department of Health, Education, and Welfare, Chicago Teacher Corps. I was responsible for coordinating the community activities of the Teacher Corps. And I worked for Upward Bound, which came out of the 1964 Economic Opportunity Act. That was part of LBJ's War on Poverty. But I went to Wright in 1969, and started doing what I had always been doing, trying to get the school to do more African American history. I would bring up people like the great historian John Hope Franklin, who was now at the University of Chicago, to lecture. Like Allison Davis before him, he wanted me to become an influential academic.

I was at Wright a few years, but my old friends and students kept saying, "What are you doing up there teaching the white kids when you should be down here?" I could see their point. And I was soon promoted, in about 1972, within the City College system to become vice president for academic affairs at Olive Harvey College, on the far South Side. I was excited about this opportunity, but I was not there long before I got a terse, surprising memo from Charles Kidd, the acting president of Olive Harvey, telling me that my position had been eliminated. He was following the orders of the chancellor of the City Colleges, Oscar Shabat, to whom I complained, demanding an explanation for my sudden dismissal. The college and chancellor soon received a great many complaints and a great deal of negative publicity—once again, my students protested, along with faculty and many others involved in the movement. Now it was "What you doin' to Prof. Black?" that they shouted. The story was everywhere, and all the bad publicity made the City Colleges rehire me—rehire me and even promote me, to a new position as director and chairperson of community affairs. In this position I had even more influence than before and could work with all the City Colleges. And I worked hard both locally and nationally to create more opportunities for black students through organizations like the National Alliance of Black School Educators and Black Faculty in Higher Education.

But this position was soon eliminated too, as part of the budget cuts in 1975. So, at that time I returned to my teaching career, teaching at Loop College, which is now appropriately named to honor Harold Washington. I taught there until my official retirement, in 1989. I like to say that I am retired, but not tired. I am not sure that the word has much meaning for me.

Still, the 1980s were another turning point, a time when my Sacred Ground again made history. Chicago was about to see some more miracles. Our Sacred Ground—Chicago's South Side—produced the personalities, the ideas, and the resources that enabled the election of Harold Washington, the city's first black mayor, in 1983.

The Meaning of Harold

I've told a lot of stories about what it was like to grow up here, how we were raised, how high the expectations were. We were also up against a lot, an awful lot. We had paid our dues, worked hard, served our country in two world wars, built businesses, and provided the nation with some of its finest and best-loved entertainment. But the city and the schools were run by men who didn't like us, and in some instances despised us, who tried to deter and confine us—literally confine us physically, as well as politically, socially, and economically. So how did it happen that, by 1983, we managed to mount a campaign that overcame racial animosity, segregation, institutional bias, election fraud, and every other sort of neglect? We elected one of our own—from our Sacred Ground—as mayor of the third-largest city in the United States. We formed relationships, built coalitions, and accomplished the "impossible," in some ways the miraculous. Within that same period, black mayors were elected in major cities around the country. But it was Chicago that paved a political road to be followed within a few years by our election of the first (and so far, the only) African American female member of the United States Senate, and later, by the first African American president of the United States.

I myself was apparently not destined for elected office, and lost another frustrating bid in the late seventies. But others were successful, and I was able to help them. I could list many names here—William Cousins, the alderman whose slogan was "unbowed, unbossed, and unbought," and who went on to become a judge, and my old friend Charlie Hayes, who succeeded Harold as a congressman and served for many years, and many others. I helped the progressive Danny Davis, on the West Side, build his successful political career.

How did it happen? Our community possessed great assets: a motherlode of talent, a deep well of creative and entrepreneurial energy, and intellectual power, all compressed in a relatively small geographic area. We grew up surrounded by cultural and commercial genius, by inventors and rebels and hard-working folk, many of whom went unheralded outside of our community (and uncompensated) during their lifetimes. We had people who had come from the South with nothing but a change of clothes and a Bible and who ended up establishing fortunes, and others who emerged as leaders by sheer force of personality and vision. I was lucky to be surrounded by such individuals. In this, I was not unusual.

Again, Harold Washington was a few years younger than me. He grew up much like I did, not at all wealthy, but aspiring. He demanded much of himself, working hard and playing hard. He came up in my neighborhood and attended my high school, DuSable. He grew up in a political household. His father, Roy Washington, was an isolated Democrat on the South Side during a period when, until 1936, most Chicago blacks were still Republicans. Like my mother, many blacks remained loyal to the party of Lincoln, until FDR came along.

Harold Washington was a true intellectual. You never saw Harold without a book. He was usually reading something serious—history, politics, science, culture. He was very easy to get to know and to talk with. Harold would have been in the first graduating class of DuSable High School. However, he didn't graduate with his class. Although he was a star athlete at DuSable, Harold grew bored with high school and dropped out in his junior year, getting a job in a meatpacking plant and later at the U.S. Treasury offices in Chicago.

When the war broke out, Harold was drafted into the army. He was part of an all-black unit (commanded by white officers) of the segregated U.S. Army Corps of Engineers. Harold served in the Pacific, building runways out on remote islands in the Philippines. He attained the rank of first sergeant.

Harold experienced harsh segregation and racist abuse within the armed forces. Like me, he came out of the military committed to a vision of full equality. He set about getting his education on the GI Bill at Roosevelt University in Chicago, where I was also a student.

A bunch of us attended Roosevelt University together in the post–World War II era. We had all attended either DuSable or Wendell Phillips, because that's where the vast majority of blacks went. We were all within a few years of each other. And now most of us were on the GI Bill. As explained earlier, Roosevelt was our college of choice because it did not discriminate or "cap" minority enrollment, and it welcomed GI Bill students. That made Roosevelt a distinctively enlightened institution, and it boasted many progressive and radical faculty members. We enjoyed the cosmopolitan atmosphere of political debate, intellectual ferment, and social equality that flourished there. We enjoyed good music, provided by the campus Jazz Club's Joe Segal, our favorite student disc jockey. (Like us, Joe was attending Roosevelt on the GI Bill. In 1947 he opened Chicago's renowned Jazz Showcase, which endures to the present day.) About half the student body was Jewish, and about an eighth of the student body was black. Roosevelt was downtown, well north of our community, and being there brought us into contact with a great variety of students. For me, it was my first time going to school with white students since my elementary school days.

By the early 1950s, we had amassed a substantial group of committed organizers and politically conscious students, including people like Bennett Johnson, who worked with me at Farragut. We became activists together at Roosevelt, and by the time we graduated, we all knew each other well. We continued to work together over the next four decades. We had a pretty tight inner group, most of whom had been friends and fellow civil rights activists since returning from the war; veterans not only of the military, but of such groups as CORE.

Harold was the leader of the Campus Young Democrats club, and that was the start of his steady rise within the mainline Democratic organization. We urged him to remain active in the Democratic Party. He was inside the machine, but not *of* the machine. He went places where many of us could not go. Harold reached across race and gender lines. People liked him very much. They responded to his warmth and humor, but also to what he projected of ethics and justice. He was an excellent debater. He loved a good argument. Harold possessed an inner fire, but he didn't lose his cool.

Among the leaders of our group were Brennetta Howell Barrett and Bennett Johnson, both then from the West Side, my old friend Oscar Brown, and Gus Savage, who later became a U.S. Congressman. By the way, Brennetta had been another, but later student of Mary Herrick, and she was at DuSable when she was inspired to a life of activism by hearing Paul Robeson perform there. They all urged Harold to remain inside the Democratic Party machine. He responded to our recommendations. We wanted someone like Harold to be positioned there within the regular Democratic organization. These activists, myself included, criticized and pushed him, and it made it possible for him to have impact on the machine itself. He recognized the need for that kind of pressure from the left. Throughout his political career he encouraged us to push and to prod him. He didn't resent it. He recognized the danger of becoming absorbed into the machine.

When he got into the Illinois legislature, the issues he promoted were issues that Daley was against. Harold's own ward boss and committeeman pushed him to give up, cave in, and shut up. Like others, he was, unfortunately, loyal to the Daley machine. So Harold actually picked up and moved from the Third Ward to the Fourth Ward, in order to have a different committeeman. He didn't need that kind of division and negative pressure. He wanted to be independent, so he got himself out from under the wing of his would-be mentor.

When Harold got to the Illinois legislature, he had important allies like Abner Mikva and Bob Mann, socially progressive, liberal Democrats who were decidedly *not* in the machine. They supported Harold on the issues in areas like education, housing, and social welfare.

Our group from Roosevelt was soon joined by others. For example, Lutrelle "Lu" Palmer, from Newport News, Virginia, moved to Chicago in 1950 to become a reporter, first at the *Chicago Defender* and then at the *Chicago Daily News*. (In the late sixties, Lu quit the *Daily News* in disgust when the editor kept altering his columns. Lu launched a small but influential newsweekly called *Black X-Press*, which lived for about a year.) We used to get together at Harold's place and stay up all night talking politics and playing poker (we mainly played for fun—whoever won had to spend the winnings buying drinks for everyone). Late at night, Harold might get a phone call, and then he'd throw us all out. His girlfriend had called. We knew she wasn't coming by to play poker. Harold's enemies spread rumors and insinuations about his sexual preferences. In those days, such talk could damage a person's reputation. Their intent was clearly to disparage and disgrace him. I don't know that Harold was bothered by that kind of talk. He expected it. He dismissed it, assuring us, "It comes with the job." He ignored it and enjoyed his life. And for the most part, the public ignored it.

Harold also liked to come to my home and visit with the family and talk politics. In the sixties, he was living on Drexel Boulevard, near my Ellis Avenue place. He felt at home with us: he would relax and play cards, laugh and eat and argue. Harold was a jocular guy but serious at the same time. He was a student of history. His jokes would be on the subtle, intellectual side. He exuded a warm and kindred feeling.

In 1968, when Dr. King was killed, Harold was in the Illinois House. He introduced a bill in the Illinois legislature to create the Martin Luther King Holiday. Illinois became the first state in the Union to create this holiday, long before it was a federal law. Harold had to gain the support of a mixed group to pass it. It took a person with the charisma, the intellect, and the political skills of a Harold Washington to make that happen. He took pride in this particular legislative accomplishment.

Harold had immense political know-how, serving in the Illinois House from 1964 until 1976, when he was elected to the Illinois Senate. Following the death of Mayor [Richard J.] Daley, Harold made an early attempt to run for mayor of Chicago in 1977. I worked hard on his campaign, but he was trounced in the Democratic primary that time around. He only carried two wards, even in his own community. But we still knew the time was getting ripe. After Daley died in office, and Wilson Frost was prevented from assuming his duties by the white politicians, the black community was coming together. Jesse Jackson brilliantly mobilized black entertainers to boycott ChicagoFest as a demonstration of black outrage at the white power structure.

After Jane Byrne won the Democratic primary for mayor of Chicago, I worked for her. She couldn't go anywhere in the black community without one of us; we decided to support her because we felt this would be an opportunity to break the old machine. I personally had to walk Jane Byrne into public housing projects and orient her and advise her on the issues. Of course when the time came for her to take office, all her appointees to the housing authority and the school board were conservative and white. Although Byrne ran as a feminist, and became the first female mayor, she was not interested in equity. African Americans remained shut out.

Meanwhile, in 1981, Harold made a successful run for the United States House of Representatives, representing the Illinois First Congressional District until his election as mayor in 1983. Now, it was during the 1980s that I served on the First Congressional District Office's Education Task Force, with local and national political implications. And because I was close to Harold, I played a role in managing his mayoral campaign, helping to register voters through groups like the People's Movement for Voter Registration and United Black Voters of Illinois.

During that period, I met Zenobia Johnson, a member of Harold's First Congressional District Housing Task Force. Zenobia was also a Chicago public school teacher, active in the A. Philip Randolph Institute, an organization addressing civil rights issues on the labor front. I did not overlook her beauty or her vivacious personality. Again, at that time I was co-chair of Harold's First Congressional District Education Task Force. Those were intense times, packed with wall-to-wall meetings, rallies, and strategy sessions. We ran countless trainings, knocked on innumerable doors. Zenobia says that we courted, married, and honeymooned during the height of the voter registration campaign and mayoral race in 1982. Happily, she recalls my being very gentlemanly and courteous in my courting of her. We've now been married for more than three decades.

Before I met Zenobia, the lasting love of my life, and after my first wife and I divorced, I was involved with some others, less happily. I was seeing someone in the late sixties who was always trying to tidy me up. She did not approve of my lifelong habit of saving everything that might be of any historical importance—my papers at the Carter G. Woodson Regional Library in the Vivian G. Harsh Research Collection of Afro-American History and Literature fill 257 boxes. There might have been more material in my papers if I had not given in to the pressure, throwing out some of my boxes of old letters—boxes that, I later discovered, included letters from Dr. King and A. Philip Randolph. My relationship with her did not last long. Neither did a second marriage of about ten years or so.

Anyway, in his brief term as a U.S. congressman, Harold made a major and historically significant contribution. He was the floor leader in the fight to extend the Voting Rights Act. He stood in the well of the House and described the tactics used by Dixiecrats and other segregationists to deter southern blacks from voting. If you listen to that list—from citizenship tests and literacy tests to poll taxes and gerrymandering and all manner of intimidation—it could easily describe the present-day methods being employed to deter black voters, and no longer are their tactics confined to the South. Harold held these practices up for national scrutiny, and his eloquent argument in support of extension won the day. He was encouraged by the Speaker of the House, Tip O'Neill.

Harold was immensely popular among his base in the First District and would easily have won reelection to Congress. However, we had other ideas.

Around 1980, Lu Palmer kicked off a new citywide group entitled Chicago Black United Communities (pronounced and known as "C-BUCK"), which aimed to get black candidates elected. He was keen on offering a real challenge to the power of the Daleys and to win city hall. CBUC's slogan was "We Shall See in '83." It was Lu's idea to enlist Harold Washington to make another run for mayor. Among all the active politicians, we agreed that Harold was the most attractive candidate, in terms of his proven skills, his composure, and his great sense of humor. He was quick-witted in a debate. And we knew where his political heart lay.

Thus, in the spring of 1982, we decided to propose that Harold become our candidate for mayor. Lu called him and asked him to come on over to the Grant Memorial Church at Forty-Fourth and Michigan Avenue. There, we asked him would he like to run for mayor. When Harold heard our proposal, his instant reaction was, "You're joking!" as if he felt it was an absurd and impossible proposal. He really didn't think it was going to happen.

Back when old man Daley (Richard J.) was the mayor, black voting in Chicago was down to about 30 percent of black adults. People were taken for granted and ignored. They were so accustomed to the official neglect, they *behaved* like they were disenfranchised. They tended to ignore the system that ignored them. Through the 1960s and 1970s, more than one third of black adults may have been registered to vote, but they did not come out and vote. Harold knew this very well. So in 1982, when we proposed that he run for mayor, he laughingly responded, "Sure—IF you get 50,000 new black voters, and raise a hundred thousand dollars, then I'll consider it." Remember, back in those days a hundred thousand dollars was like a million bucks today.

What Harold understood was that we would have to break through. It was not that black folks were apathetic. They were, however, accustomed to a certain way of being treated, of being governed. We would need an awakened community. We would need strong alliances, because we knew we were facing strong, entrenched opposition. We knew there were other communities that were similarly disenfranchised. Harold knew it too. He challenged us to demonstrate that we could out-organize the old machine.

He figured it was a safe bet. Little did he imagine how far we would exceed his challenge.

We had Renault Robinson, the founder of the Afro-American Patrolmen's League, with us. Robinson was widely respected. He was a gifted organizer. He was a known, public opponent of racism, graft, and police brutality. At one point we were even considering Renault as our candidate for mayor. Had Harold not agreed to run, Renault would likely have been our next choice for a candidate. But now, in answer to Harold's challenge, we had to figure out how to raise some quick money.

I recruited Renault to come with me to talk to Ed Gardner, one of the wealthiest individuals I knew, to ask for financial help. I didn't comprehend quite how very rich Ed was, though I had known him a long time. Ed had graduated from Fenger High School, and his wife Bettiann had graduated from DuSable High School. Ed became a Chicago public school teacher after the war, and later an administrator. During the early 1960s, he and his wife started a black hair-care company out of their home. Ed was now the founder and owner of Soft Sheen Products, one of the two major black-owned companies manufacturing and selling a line of hair products targeting black men and women. They claimed they tested their products out first on the family dog. By the early 1980s, Soft Sheen was doing more than $55 million a year in sales. And this started from a basement kitchen in the home of a guy who lived in my neighborhood and attended a Chicago public school.

Ed immediately saw the importance of careful organizing for a black mayoral campaign, whoever the candidate might turn out to be. He told us, "I pledge to donate my entire September advertising budget to voter registration, a quarter of a million dollars."

As soon as that decision was made, we went into action. We launched a campaign with a very public deadline, to make sure we could get it done in time for Harold to commit fully to running for mayor. We were able to open an office and hire a staff of trainers to recruit many volunteers. We put in position a network of organizers, and produced a supply of publications and posters in a variety of languages. We partnered up with a Hispanic voter organization based in Pilsen. Several leaders among Puerto Rican and Mexican neighborhoods began to sit with us to figure out how to mobilize our respective bases. Among these were Rudy Lozano, a talented young labor organizer from Pilsen; Luis Gutiérrez, who went on to become a U.S. congressman from Humboldt Park; and Jesús "Chuy" García, a youthful community organizer from Little Village who is today a Cook County elected official and mayoral contender. We also formed a coalition with community organizers on the city's North and Northwest Sides—among them Walter "Slim" Coleman and Helen Shiller, leaders in what was at that time a predominantly low-income white section of the city. Shiller went on to become a twenty-year member of the city council.

With Ed Gardner's help we were able to plaster the South and West Sides with posters, stickers, and literature. We trained hundreds of voter registrars and canvassers. We put voter registration materials and registrars into barbershops, mom-and-pop stores, and of course, churches. We held open-air rallies and voter registration drives at every big event—parades, picnics, concerts.

Under the banner "Come Alive October 5," we registered more than two hundred thousand voters by our self-imposed deadline of October 5, 1982, and then we registered another sixty-three thousand more. It was the single biggest voter registration campaign ever conducted in the history of the country—and, I believe, the most successful in all previous history for any particular group in an urban area anywhere. We had met Harold's dare more than fivefold. We celebrated this success, but we didn't stop to rest.

Ed Gardner, our initial benefactor, got together with the other two dominant leaders of the black business world at that time. He approached John Johnson, the owner of Johnson Publishing, the publishers of *Ebony* and *Jet*, and real estate magnate Dempsey Travis. The three of them proceeded to round up the rest of the black business community—bankers, car dealers, gas station owners, insurance executives, and the like. They raised more than a million dollars—ten times the amount that Harold had challenged us to raise. In today's campaign money, that would be small change, but in 1982, it was an astronomical sum.

So I was able to go back to Harold. "Well," I said, "what you gonna do now, man?" Harold smiled that slow smile of his, and he told me, "Well . . . I guess I'm gonna run." Our campaign tapped the deep discontent among the low-income sections of the city, particularly on the South and West Sides, and among others who were disheartened by the city's institutional segregation and police abuses. Not only were people interested in the campaign, they had confidence in its leaders. We had tapped into a strong current of desire for change, for a new image for Chicago, for new opportunities, and for a more open city.

When Harold spoke, he evoked that vision in his audiences. After winning the primary—because Byrne and Daley (Richard M., Daley the Younger) split the white vote—he found himself running against a candidate who was selected for no other reason than race. Bernard Epton, a white Hyde Park resident, became the nominee of the Republican Party. The campaign slogan was "Anyone but Harold." They might as well have said, "Anyone but the Black Guy." (And that's putting it in the least obnoxious terms.)

During the Democratic primary, Daley was caught on camera addressing a group of elderly white Northwest Side residents, telling them why they should vote for him in the simplest of terms: "You want a white mayor." (When confronted, Daley claimed he was misunderstood. He swore that he said, "You want a wet mayor.") The gloves were off, and it took a strong stomach to campaign, what with the racial heckling, the destruction of campaign signs, and the disruption of rallies and meetings. We held each other up with strong feelings of fellowship and a sense of mission that would not be denied.

What was my role in Harold's election? Honestly, my role was to teach people how to get organized and to help craft the platform on which Harold ran, and to work organizing young people—high school and college students—to carry out voter registration. I identified a lot of talented young organizers who took big slices of the city, people who had been organizing in Uptown, in Humboldt Park, in Pilsen, and on the North Side. Not just on the South and West Sides. We kept careful records of who lived where, who was registered, who was with us, and who was on the fence. When it came time to get out the vote, we would be ready. We were—there was a record voter turnout of 79 percent, with Harold winning 98 percent of the black vote.

After Harold became the mayor, I continued supporting him and promoting his importance as a person dedicated to the welfare of the entire city, not just to people of color. He asked me what job I wanted. I wasn't looking for a job—I was glad enough to be teaching at the City College that would later be named after him. He offered me a seat on the Streets and Sanitation commission. I figured that at least I could help the neighborhoods if I served on Streets and San. Help clean it up. Have an ear on what was going on. Harold nominated me to become a commissioner, but my effort to become the chairman had to be approved by the city council. I lacked the support of the members who were part of the Regular Democratic Organization. Without machine support, I didn't have a chance. I served as a commissioner from 1983 to 1987, but after Harold's death I was unseated as a commissioner. So much for my foray into the byzantine world of paving, rodent control, sewer maintenance, and garbage removal.

Harold accomplished several major initiatives despite incomparable obstructionism from the "Vrdolyak 29." This was a bloc of city council members named for its leader, a vicious alderman by the name of Ed Vrdolyak. With just a slight majority in the fifty-member council, the twenty-nine banded together in a racist cabal to try to block all of Harold's appointments, budgetary changes, reforms of all sorts that his administration might put forth. Some observers were shocked by the level of malice manifest in the behavior of the racist opposition during what became known as "Council Wars." I was not shocked in the least. I had grown up around this type of racism.

Harold managed to wear them down and was able to appoint African Americans in the leadership of the Chicago Police Department, the Housing Authority, and the Chicago Public Schools system. None of these appointments happened without fierce challenges from his opponents. He initiated massive public meetings to discuss the future of the Chicago public schools. The Education Summit brought together thousands of parents, teachers, and community leaders to demand adequate funding, a real end to school segregation, and a greater role for parents and teachers in the management of the public schools. It led to the most sweeping school reform legislation in the country for that time.

I tried to advise his people that Harold had to spend more time in the community that helped to elect him. When you looked at the figures, you could see we had such a massive outpouring of Latino and black voters. So my role was to support him as much as I could. Yet once he took office, we hardly ever got together. As sometimes happens when people get elected to higher office, Harold became more difficult to contact. But Harold began to realize that many of those people surrounding him were not necessarily loyal to him or to the movement which elected him, but were loyal to the establishment, to the status quo. Harold began to do much of the outreach work himself.

I confess that I felt a bit hurt and disappointed not to have greater access to Harold, not to have his ear, like I used to have when we sat up and talked politics on our poker nights. He was surrounded by handlers and managers, the gatekeepers; indeed, some of the very same ones who surrounded President Obama when he was in office. I feared that Harold's popular base that we had worked so hard to mobilize was eroding very quickly. Some of his original stalwart supporters, like Lu and his wife Jorja Palmer, who had been in the inner circle of the campaign, felt very put out. They felt that Harold failed to listen to all our voices. They had to be convinced to continue to support Harold. But we did, and he won a second term.

Shortly before Harold's sudden death in November of 1987, I had a chance to talk with him. He was being honored, along with gospel music producer Sid Ordower, a staunch Washington supporter. The occasion was the annual dinner of the Chicago Committee to Defend the Bill of Rights, and Jesús "Chuy" García was the keynote speaker. I went over to shake Harold's hand, and he greeted me with a bear hug. "Hey, Tim," he said to me, "where ya been? Why don't you ever call me?" I told him I'd tried to, but couldn't get past his handlers. He replied, "Well, let's get together and catch up." I told him of my concern for his health. "You've got to take better care of yourself," I said, and he said he knew it too. He told me to call his secretary and get scheduled in for a meeting. That was the last time I saw him. He dropped dead of a massive heart attack just a few days later. The black community was plunged into a palpable grief, as was much of the rest of the city.

I was in my office at Loop College when someone said, "Mr. Black, the mayor just died!" I was talking with a young Chinese student of mine, and she just started crying and said "Oh my God!" I tried to comfort her before going to teach my class. I went to meet with my class, but found that I had to stop the class to let the students grieve—my students were overwhelmingly for Harold, and many had worked on his campaign. I talked to them about the difference they had made in getting him elected. But it was so hard to accept that Harold was dead, and there would be no more campaigning for him.

But while it thrived, the Washington campaign and its victory created the same kind of excitement on the local level that Barack Obama's would generate on the national level two decades later. It taught so many younger people about the power of an awakened, organized community. It was the students who insisted on changing the name of Loop College to Harold Washington College.

I didn't approve of everything Harold did, but I certainly approved of most of what he did. He was a good mayor for all the people. I was proud to call him a friend and proud to have played a part in the breakthrough that his election represented. And I remain proud of our community, which produced him, and all it has meant for our city. I hope Chicago learned something.

CHAPTER 5

Talking to the Elders

My memories of Harold are some of the most vivid memories I have of the 1980s. He was such a powerful, inspiring figure, and such a great friend, that I cannot adequately express what his loss meant to me and to my community, my Sacred Ground. After his death, so much of our activism came to a halt, though not in any organized fashion, and despite the efforts of dedicated activists like Jesse Jackson. Somehow we lost the feeling, the unity.

I had worked hard for Rev. Jesse Jackson Sr. in his presidential campaigns, in 1984 and 1988. He was a brilliant speaker, and on the issues I found little to disagree with. In fact, polls showed that most Americans actually agreed with him on the key issues—when those issues were presented without being associated with him. But racism, then as now, was such a strong force that too many people could not get over their prejudices even to support the candidate who would best serve their interests. Despite his strong showing in a number of primaries, it was clear that the country was not yet ready to elect a black president. So, the letdown after those campaigns and the death of Harold was pretty devastating.

It was only about half a year or so after Harold's death that we renamed Loop College Harold Washington College, in his honor. That was an appropriate honor—Harold believed in educational opportunities like those afforded by the City Colleges. And by time, I was nearing seventy years of age and decided that it was about time for me to retire. I still loved teaching. I loved trying to inspire my young students to keep on keepin' on, and to remember that trouble don't last forever. But the movement was in a difficult period, and I was developing some new interests.

At Loop College, I was professor of anthropology, cultural anthropology, sociology, and history, and although I was always teaching black history, I found myself more and more thinking about how to preserve that history as I had experienced it, how to preserve the stories that the elders had to tell. For so many generations, black people had learned from our elders, the way I had learned from my grandmother, and it always troubled me when young people acted like everything began with them. "What was ain't no is no mo" my ex-slave grandmother used to say. Those words always seemed like a call to listen and remember. It seemed to me that both our physical history, the spaces and places of my Sacred Ground, and our spiritual history, our stories and memories, were being systematically destroyed. We watched Bronzeville change. We saw the wrecking ball take down the old Regal Theater, the Savoy, and so many other places of my youth. With those places, and others, Forty-Seventh Street at what is now King Drive used to be the center of the universe: if you were looking for a black person in Chicago, all you had to do was stand there awhile and they would come by, the rich and the poor, the famous and the typical old hoodlums like me. But after the end of restrictive covenants, and with the destruction wrought by urban renewal (often rightly called "Negro Removal" and supported by the University of Chicago), along with the concentration of low-income people in high-rise housing projects, things changed. Changed too quickly. The class conflicts that came with the second Great Migration meant that now young people in Bronzeville were not growing up with doctors and lawyers and other successful people around them, the way I did. Those successful people were moving out. How ironic is it that the old Regal Theater was demolished in 1973 and later replaced with the Harold Washington Cultural Center? I am glad to see Harold honored that way, but I am saddened by the loss of those grand old buildings and the social change that reflects.

This destruction has been chronicled by many brilliant young scholars. I admire their work and am so grateful to them for all that they have done. But those of us who lived through the changes, who experienced firsthand the loss of our history, our Sacred Ground, can help tell that history from our angles, as participants. Len Despres and others, like my old student Harold Lucas, appreciated the importance of architectural preservation, of how you could destroy a people, destroy their history, by destroying their historic buildings. We have saved many, like the Rosenwald building, named after Julius Rosenwald, the Sears executive who was a great philanthropist and supporter of the South Side arts. That building was home to so many of the famous residents of Bronzeville. But this struggle always continues. The places that remain, places like Burke Elementary, DuSable High School (now a group of charter schools), the Wabash YMCA, the Liberty Life building, the Eighth Regiment Armory (now a military academy), the South Side Community Art Center, and, across the street, the home of my friend the great Margaret Burroughs, the artist who founded the DuSable Museum of African American History right there in her living room—these places are now invaluable, part of the cultural legacy of Bronzeville that we cannot afford to lose. I have supported all of them, and my long association with the DuSable Museum, and Margaret Burroughs, has helped me appreciate the crucial work of preservation, work often carried on as well by former students such as Harold and friends like Bernard Turner and Sherry Williams.

But during my years at Loop College, I started thinking more and more about the spiritual history of Bronzeville, about how important it was to talk to the elders, to hear and record their stories, so that this side of our history would not be lost. I was in a good position to be a participant observer and to use some of the methods of cultural anthropology, the field techniques that would allow people to tell their own stories their own way. This was important.

I was also pushed by my two children. I was and am very proud of them. They excelled in their educations, with Ermetra going to Bennington and Timuel Kerrigan to Stanford, and then the Berkeley School of Folklore. As I recorded in the introduction to the first volume of *Bridges*, they came to me one day and said, "Dad, you have been so active and done so much, why don't you write a book about your life?" Then they handed me a legal pad and pen and told me to get started. But while I was still teaching at Loop College that was not very practical advice. But I did decide, in 1988, that I would somehow record and preserve the recollections of people who had grown up and lived in that area I call Sacred Ground. Then, at my retirement dinner in March of 1989, my fellow members of the Black Faculty in Higher Education issued me a check and a challenge to go ahead and write the book.

I bought an old word processor and started what I knew would be a very long and difficult project. But as I also noted in that introduction, sadly, the project became more urgent because of the death of my son. He was a brilliant young man, a musical prodigy who was making his living in the Bay Area as a musician, composer, and producer of one-man shows, especially for young people. He had even put together and developed an original one-man show called "Tryin' to Get Home," which was based on African American songs and highlighted black history. He was carrying on that love of music, and belief in the importance of music in the struggle for social justice and a better world, that I described earlier in this book. He was gay, and when he revealed to me that his HIV infection had turned into AIDS, at a time when the drugs for treating it were not available, and the tragic situation was all too clear, he tried to lighten our moods by asking, "Dad, how are you coming along with that book?" He died from kidney failure due to AIDS on March 8, 1993. The National Task Force on AIDS Prevention later produced a video of his work "Children of the Night" to encourage safe sex among gay black men. I realized that I had to finish my oral history project because I had promised him that I would. He was a fine son, and I will always miss him so much and cherish his memory.

Sadness and personal loss would also strike later that decade, in 1999, when my older brother Walter passed. He was eighty-four, and living in the Renaissance Nursing Home, but he was always jovial, a grand person with whom I shared so much of both the physical and spiritual life of our Sacred Ground. He had achieved such prominence in his life that the Illinois House of Representatives even passed the following resolution:

HOUSE RESOLUTION

WHEREAS, The members of the Illinois House of Representatives are saddened to learn of the death of Walter Kerrigan Black, who recently passed away; and

WHEREAS, Walter Black was born in Birmingham, Alabama, on January 27, 1915; his parents were Timuel D. and Mattie McConner Black; the family moved to the south side of Chicago in 1918, and young Walter attended Burke Elementary School and Tilden High School; during the years of the Depression, Walter dropped out of school to help support his family; he returned to

Tilden and was co-captain of the basketball team, standing with his teammates when they won the 1935 City Championship; as a result of winning an essay contest that same year, Walter won a Legislative Scholarship, choosing to attend the University of Illinois; and

WHEREAS, Walter Black studied political science and history at the U of I; he was one of but a few black students on the large campus, and found his activities limited due to the prejudices of the time; in 1939 he graduated from the University of Illinois and moved to Milwaukee; he went to work for the Greenbaum Tannery, where he also played basketball; and

WHEREAS, Walter Black went into the United States Army in 1942; he received basic training at Camp Butner in North Carolina, then went on to serve his county in England and Austria during World War II; and

WHEREAS, Taking advantage of the G.I. Bill, Walter Black attended and studied at John Marshall Law School; while attending school he clerked under Attorney Fleetwood McCoy; upon graduation, he passed the Bar Exam on his first try; he took a job in the legal firm of McCoy, Ming, and Leighton, and was made a partner in 1952; he worked on many important cases as an attorney, including representing Fuller Products and saving the company from bankruptcy; together with his partner Robert Ming, Walter Black helped Richard Hatcher become the first black mayor of Gary, Indiana; and

WHEREAS, Walter Black is survived by his brother, Timuel (Zenobia); his niece, Ermetra Black-Thomas (Maurice); his many cousins; and many colleagues and friends; therefore, be it

RESOLVED, BY THE HOUSE OF REPRESENTATIVES OF THE NINETY-FIRST GENERAL ASSEMBLY OF THE STATE OF ILLINOIS, that we mourn, along with his family and friends, the death of Walter Black; may all that knew him find comfort in this time of need; and be it further

RESOLVED, That a suitable copy of this resolution be presented to the family of Walter Black.

These tragic experiences made the job of finishing my oral history project take on a real urgency. So I set about the work, planning a series of interviews with a relatively large number of people who grew up in my community. I was inspired in part by the oral histories of my old friend Studs Terkel, who supported my work and even contributed a foreword to the first volume. John Hope Franklin also honored me by contributing a foreword. I wanted to interview a wide range of people who were articulate and could describe their struggles and experiences growing up in Chicago. Again, as I put it in the first volume, the purpose was to create a full and representative range of subjective information that all of us can review, examine, criticize, modify, or even reject. But this process of personal evaluation may serve to help the present and future generations understand the distinctive qualities of the individual lives as well as the collective life of black folk in Chicago, whether it be organized, unorganized, or even disorganized. The same applies to the present work. Whatever its flaws, this is the way I remember it. These are the memories that "crowd the corners of my mind." This is primary source material.

Because it has turned out to be such an important part of my life, my work doing oral history calls for some more explanation, an account of why, for me, oral history is the "real deal." As noted, the books which represent several years' worth of my life work are entitled *Bridges of Memory*, and there are to date two volumes, detailing the lives of participants in Chicago's first wave of the Great Migration—those who, like me, arrived here from the South, many of them from my generation, who were brought here as children; and even some who arrived here at a relatively mature age. For these books, I interviewed dozens of these individuals extensively, recorded their responses, asked probing questions, and helped them to recollect in part because I share common memories with them. My aim was to create through their memories and stories a picture of life in my Sacred Ground in its early years and onward.

Within the academic world there is more than one attitude toward what we call oral history. I'm referring to the history handed down through our oral tradition. In slave times and afterward, it was prohibited to teach black persons to read and write. But they could never stop us from telling our stories and passing them down in spoken form, in sung form, even by means of the drums. In some quarters, there is a sort of snobbery toward oral history because it does not flow from a base of academic scholarship or archeological research. It flows from folklore, from family lore, and from the memories of those who lived it or heard it from their elders. Oral history is what I collected from scores of black

Chicago residents of the South Side. I did not seek to verify their stories through archival research. I attempted to create an atmosphere of trust in which my interview subjects could relax and remember, sometimes cheerfully and sometimes tearfully, depending on what we were recalling. For each of my subjects, our understanding was that we were getting together in order to make a historical record based on their lives and experiences. Something that their children and grandchildren might read and understand. This was the sole incentive for them to participate.

Now, Studs Terkel was my dear friend and brother, and a big influence on my ideas. He was a fellow social activist, as well as an entertainer, commentator, critic, prolific writer, and agitator. He used his considerable skills as an interviewer to draw out people's stories—some of them painful, some of them triumphant. He would select a theme or a historical event or a period of time or a neighborhood (like Chicago's Division Street) to investigate through the voices of ordinary people who had lived through the events or lived in the neighborhood, or worked at a job, or fought in a war. Studs loved jazz and so he collected oral histories of jazz musicians. In his later years, Studs explored people's ideas about getting old and about facing death.

When we filled up that train to Washington, D.C., in the summer of 1963, with people heading to the March for Jobs and Freedom, Studs brought his tape recorder and rode the train. He could have gone by airplane. But, he told me, that would not have given him enough time to talk to the passengers and inquire about their reasons for going to the March. On the overnight train ride, he recorded dozens of interviews. They were preserved as part of the documentary record of the civil rights movement. Studs talked to everybody—the kids, the Pullman porters, the other journalists, about the March on Washington. All the way to Washington he kept moving up and down the aisles.

We were good friends. Studs grew up on Chicago's North Side and I grew up on the South Side, but he had the same love of his old neighborhood as I had of mine, and he knew a million stories. He had a bear trap of a memory. He could tell you details about yourself or your family that you might have forgotten. He was a loyal pal.

On his ninetieth birthday, in 2002, the Chicago Historical Society was the site of a birthday celebration for Studs. I was one of the many speakers. The master of ceremonies was Rick Kogan, the journalist. Rick's a good guy, but when the time came in the proceedings for him to introduce me, he said something along the lines of, "Let me introduce Tim Black, otherwise known as 'The Black Studs Terkel.'" Well, that went over like a lead balloon. The audience did not laugh uproariously. But Studs jumped up, grabbed the microphone from Rick, and quipped, "I prefer to think of myself as the white Timuel Black!" Now they laughed. Studs humorized an awkward moment and saved the day.

We respected each other. We learned from each other. I was a subject of Studs's interviews in several of his books, and I always felt that he had the best ear. He listened hard, he laughed often, and he recorded diligently. I feel like one thing I learned from watching him work was to truly and accurately represent what people said to him, not to put the words in their mouths that he might have preferred them to say. Not to misuse their stories or alter them. Now, it's one thing to shorten things up or avoid offensive language . . . but he was a master at this craft of collecting stories. So I'd say Studs was a social historian with an original style and a true humanist.

My own training in social sciences was formalistic, academic, and I guess you'd say classical. At Roosevelt University as an undergrad, I observed and learned from the great social scientist St. Clair Drake. He was my professor and academic mentor. And in terms of style and methodology you could say both St. Clair Drake and Terkel were my major influences. They were both interested in the historical context and world events that shaped the outlook of the people they studied. They both had deep respect for the communities and individuals whose lives they investigated.

But Studs always encouraged me to pursue oral history. "These stories are out there waiting for us. Let's go get 'em." To those who consider oral history "soft" history, or somehow less valid, I would say, it's the people who are left out of history whose stories we are collecting and saving. They are not emperors or movie stars, but they have stories that give us understanding. Oral history deserves the respect that is given to the more classical forms and methods.

I was honored in the spring of 2005 to pinch-hit for Studs at a prestigious academic conference. The annual meeting of the American Educational Research Association came to Chicago, and Studs was scheduled to give a major talk about oral history. The session was entitled "Listening and Teaching." Hundreds of people were expected at this event, but on the day of it, Studs was not feeling well. So he asked me to take his place. "But Studs," I said, "they're expecting to see YOU. They won't know me from Adam." Studs urged me to just go in there and talk about history and tell them some stories about the Chicago they would not learn about from being downtown at the Hyatt Regency. Stories I had gathered from my own interviews.

When it was announced that Studs Terkel would not be speaking, probably half the disappointed audience got up and walked out of the auditorium. But there were still a couple hundred people who remained, and I did manage to give them a talk mixing teaching, learning, and community history. They kept listening, so I kept talking. It was about two hours of storytelling. I have my standard stories that I tell—the ones included in this book. I have my song lyrics and my jokes that I tell to lighten up some of the difficult parts. Drawing on my teaching career, I told the story of Bill Daniels, since his success story is extraordinary and inspiring, and the message got through to the audience. Don't underestimate your students' intellectual capacity or their potential. Don't go by a single yardstick in imagining how far they can go in life. And the second, equally serious message to these educational researchers was that we all can be researchers, we all can be listeners, we can teach our children the skills of oral history. They can interview their own grandparents, their neighbors, to collect images and stories that depict life. It can be preparation for more mature qualitative research, for political insight, for community organizing.

This kind of active inquiry, listening and recording, is a wonderful teaching method that I feel is a bit neglected. We tend to teach history in the conventional way of demanding that children memorize the dates that events happened and the names of the presidents in the correct order, and other facts. But without context, these are random and not meaningful to children, and they are not likely to be retained in memory without color, without personalities, without stories.

As things turned out, the teachers and researchers liked what I had to convey. Oral history is not the stepchild of the discipline of history. It is beginning to get the recognition it ought always to have received. In 2011, the Oral History Association honored me at their annual meeting. This is the preeminent body of historians who tend to share my view of the legitimacy and the validity of oral history as a discipline. It is not random or fly-by-night. It has its ethical principles, standards, and practices, and the field is growing. Now there are oral history courses at many major universities internationally. At the 2011 event, the professional organization of oral historians gave me a special award acknowledging *Bridges of Memory* and my work as an activist, not as contradictory but as a worthy combination. I was particularly touched that the OHA characterized *Bridges of Memory* as "a people's history of Black Chicago."

Yet I know that in the case of my anthologies of oral history interviews, some scholars view them as interesting resources, but perhaps don't regard them as serious scholarship. What can I say about this? These are the firsthand accounts of people who lived through the Great Migration, many of them the first generation after slavery, talking about why their families left the South, what they left behind, how their families survived in the new surroundings of Chicago. They offer reflections on the good, the bad, and the ugly, the successes and defeats they experienced here. They cannot be dismissed. Similarly, this memoir is my own personal story. I am not attempting to be comprehensive on the entire history of the city, nor even of my own life. I have so many stories, I've known so many personalities, that I could not possibly put it all into this memoir. But I'm telling stories that I hope capture a feeling, a spirit of what this place and its people have meant, not just to me, but to our city and our country. First-person story-telling seems to me the most accessible, plain-spoken, and true way to paint that picture. For me, and I hope for you, oral history is the real deal.

Again, with *Bridges*, since I had known most of the people I interviewed for a long time, and they felt comfortable talking to me, the conversations also seemed like gossipy conversations between old friends. That added to their value. I wanted the people I was interviewing to talk freely and candidly; they might get this or that fact wrong, but this is how they remembered it. Because of this quality in the conversations, they also conveyed a lot about me and my life on this Sacred Ground. My speaking freely helped my interviewees speak freely.

The plan was to do a first volume featuring interviews with people of the first Great Migration, and then a second volume with interviews with people from the next generation, their children and others, with a third volume that would carry the story forward to their children. So far, two volumes have appeared, though they do not have a strict chronological order. The third volume is still in preparation, though at my age, it cannot be delayed much longer.

I could. By the way, did you ever know Mrs. Frances Berry? She was a clerk at our library in DuSable.

TB: She was there later on when I taught at DuSable, and I remember that she was very nice, and I could always depend on her to take good care of the students that I sent to the library for special assignments. You know, I hated to leave that school when I did, but the principal at that time and I didn't get along so well.

IC: Who was the principal then?

TB: Mrs. Stack, and I understand that she and Mary Herrick, they didn't get along so well either.

(*Bridges*, vol. 1, 139–40)

Mary Herrick came up again in the enjoyable conversation that I had with my friend Jimmy Ellis, the saxophonist and music teacher. I met him in 1970, when he was very concerned about the black musicians union merging with the white one. He turned out to be right about that. His older brother Morris, also featured in *Bridges*, was one of the most popular bandleaders in Chicago. Both of them studied at DuSable with Captain Dyett:

TB: Now, at that time, when they graduated from DuSable, they were already good musicians.

JE: I think that's because Walter Dyett, the music teacher there at DuSable, had the awareness to know that, "Hey, I don't care if you don't like me. If you want to play the horn, then you've got to practice and do just what I say." So he wasn't soft. Total discipline was required.

TB: I know that.

JE: And you've got not only to be able to play the music—it's also how you looked, how you dressed—everything. "Whatever you're doing, if it's not in order, get out of here."

TB: I remember coming down the hall one day, and I said to myself, "Gee, how can everybody stay in that man's class?" But guys would be begging to get back in after he had put them out!

JE: And he only had one eye. The other eye was a glass eye, so a person wasn't always sure if he was talking to them. He'd say, "Get out of here!" and they'd say, "You talking to me?" and he'd say, "Yeah!"

[*Laughter.*]

TB: Oh, Cap [Dyett] was something else!

JE: Yes, but Walter Dyett was never a person who would stand off. Even during his lunch he would come over and talk to you. He was always a part of what you were doing. He was very strict, but he was not the type of person to pass by you and not talk to you or whatever.

TB: He was always friendly, but I just knew he was strict, and I used to wonder, "How does everybody take what he's putting down?"

JE: Well, if you don't learn that kind of discipline, they run over you.

TB: Getting ready for "Hi-Jinks" at DuSable was really an event, wasn't it?

JE: Well, Captain would teach school during the day, and then he would have to come back at night to rehearse for "Hi-Jinks." You've got the stage crew, the manager, the costumes—he put that whole thing together. And everybody learned something through it. It wasn't just the band. It was the whole production. Do you remember Johnny Hauser?

TB: Yes.

JE: Well, he was my private teacher. He was beautiful. And as a matter of fact, I did my practice teaching with him, but if it hadn't been for Walter Dyett, I don't know where I'd be today.

TB: We need to make a special fund for him—like we did for Miss Herrick. You remember Miss Mary Herrick?

JE: Yes, of course, I remember Miss Herrick.

TB: Now, we make contributions to the school in her name, and they provide for some small scholarships. Every year. The same thing should apply to those of you who knew Dyett.

JE: That's right.

(*Bridges*, vol. 1, 166–67)

Now, when I interviewed Morris, he too went on about the importance of Captain Dyett. I had known Morris for over forty years, and I was glad that he captured that spirit of community that we grew up with:

ME: Well, we grew up at Forty-Ninth and Champlain, right behind Willard School, so I went to Willard School for eight years.

TB: That was the old Grand Boulevard neighborhood.

ME: Yes, and the area we lived in was called "The Valley." It sort of had a slope downwards, and then, after graduating from Willard School, I went to DuSable High School for four years.

TB: What was that neighborhood like when you were growing up?

ME: It was a real community. A community where everybody knew everybody else. Everybody *cared* about everybody, and there was no such thing as "you belong to somebody else." It was, "You belong to *me*." Every adult on that block knew me and knew my family, plus my mother had an open-house policy anyway. If any of the adults in the whole community saw Morris Ellis doing something wrong, they had the right to chastise him—mentally, physically, whatever. And they would tell my folks! They'd call them up and take me back home! So, it was one of those situations where I didn't get into too much trouble. I was too busy trying to learn how to play my little horn. I started playing the horn when I was in grammar school, even though I don't think I really mastered it until I was at DuSable.

(*Bridges*, vol. 1, 177).

That was my experience too. It was part of that typical experience of our Sacred Ground, and similar accounts of the closeness of our community come up in almost every interview in *Bridges*. Sometimes this was even referring to other parts of Chicago, as in my interview with the great Jerry "Iceman" Butler, the rhythm and blues pioneer who went on to a political career and became a Cook County commissioner: "Yes, where are the 'Pearl's Kitchens' of today? They have all been replaced by the McDonald's and the Kentucky Fried Chicken type of places where you just go in, grab the food, and take it on out. People used to sit down in the places where they ate and have conversations there. You know, the most wonderful thing about Pearl's Kitchen was that you'd hear all sorts of people speaking with each other. You'd hear preachers talking to gamblers. There was a mutual understanding that even though I can't convince you that my philosophy is right or that your philosophy is wrong, we can still have an interesting and informative conversation with each other." I added, "People were able to communicate with each other like that because there was mutual understanding and respect" (*Bridges*, vol. 2, 183–84). Jerry had grown up on the Near North Side.

Some of the people interviewed in the second volume of *Bridges* are older than some of those who appeared in the first volume. The Reverend Dr. Lou Rawls, whose Tabernacle Missionary Baptist Church at 4130 South Indiana featured everyone from Paul Robeson to A. Philip Randolph, Fannie Lou Hamer, Mahalia Jackson, and Dr. King, was born in Mississippi in 1904. The Reverend A. P. Jackson, who was a friend of Dr. King's and made his church, Liberty Baptist, available to Dr. King on many occasions, was my age. And my old friend Rudy Nimocks, who had a career as a detective with the Chicago Police Department before heading the University of Chicago Police Department and later becoming an ambassador for their Office of Civic Engagement, could have been in the second volume instead of the first. Anyway, I enjoyed doing all of the interviews, for both volumes, and am so grateful to all of those people for taking the time to talk to me. These conversations helped me recollect and record so many things that should not be forgotten, such as the role of David Kellum, Mr. "Bud Billiken," in starting the Bud Billiken parade, an event that no aspiring South Side politician can afford to miss. And I enjoyed this exchange with Justice William Cousins, referring to our work in the 1960s and how Mayor Daley (Richard J.) was always trying to buy people off:

> **TB:** Well, while I never attained the status of an elected office, the mayor had folks chasing after me because he didn't want a straggling voice out there against him. He wanted it to be closed off. And, then, of course, he made an example of people whom he could bring in so he could say, "See, they can all be bought." And that sort of thing discourages people, particularly young people. When they have given some admiration to certain people, and then they

see those people drop by the wayside, things like that decrease the young people's ability to resist the forces of evil. So Daley sent a few people my way, and I handled it just like you did. Ed Marciniak called me and said, "The mayor wants to see you."

WC: Yes, he was the mayor's main man for a long time.

TB: Well, this was after the mayor got booed off the stand in 1963. The mayor thought I had something to do with it, and he was right. But I said, "Well, we'll be down." And he said, "No, just you." And I said, "No, I can't come to see the mayor by myself. No." And so the meeting never happened. But then, of course, he sent one of his other agents over to me to plead his case.

WC: In the whole scheme of things, you know, respect and honor really outrank everything else.

TB: Yes, and part of that is self-respect.

WC: Oh, yes, you have to have self-respect. If you have self-respect, then you have the respect of others. That surely is more valuable than all of these other things.

(*Bridges*, vol. 1, 523–24)

When I reflect on those conversations, I see how revealing they were of my own deepest convictions, as well as, I hope, those of my interviewees. But one of the interviews in the second volume, one of those with a younger person, a former student of mine at Hyde Park, has some special significance for me. Jesse Brown was my student, and he became a decorated Vietnam War hero. He was wounded in the war. When he returned to the U.S. he became the executive director of Disabled American Veterans, before becoming secretary of veterans affairs. He was only fifty-eight when he died, in 2002, of Lou Gehrig's disease. I was so honored to interview this young man, who was a true leader. But he wanted to talk about me:

JB: The thing that I most remember about you as a teacher was that you made us feel proud of ourselves. You brought a new dimension into our lives because you taught us to have self-respect and helped us to learn that we as a people don't have any reason to be ashamed of who we are or apologize to anyone for the way that we look. You know it really bothers me today when I see these young boys with their hair all processed and all that stuff because it suggests to me that they want to defy nature in order to look more like someone that they can never ever or should never look like. For example, take Michael Jackson. He is all screwed up trying to look white. He has messed up his hair, his skin, his facial features, and everything else in order to look like something that he can never be. What a lot of people like him don't seem to understand is that we don't need to be running around trying to look or act like somebody else. We need to be proud of who we are.

TB: It's like Elie Wiesel said when somebody said to him, "You are white. Why don't you just become a gentile? Why don't you just stop being Jewish?" His answer was, "What? Betray my ancestors, my great-grandparents, my whole history, betray all of that? No, I can't do that. I don't need to be a gentile. I need to be Elie Wiesel." Of course I take that same position. All of my grandparents were slaves. My mother was kind of fair-skinned, but none of my relatives ever professed to be anything but black. My daddy was a strong black man. He is my hero. I don't need no other hero to be my inspiration. All the rest of the heroes have to ride on his back! My mama was a strong black woman who carried us in comfort through the Depression. For me to try and transfer my allegiance to some other group would be like Elie Wiesel deciding not to be Jewish. Being who I am is my foundation, and I will go down in defeat, if it is necessary, proclaiming the legitimacy of that heritage!

JB: What's more is that if you attempt to deny your heritage, you will automatically fail in whatever it is you have chosen to do.

TB: And the reason for that is that once you have decided that you want to look like someone else or act like them, then you are also going to try to think like them and accept their limitations as your own. You are going to think that they have all the answers, but the answers for you are not out there. Those answers are in you! Once you get that straight, your confidence level moves up, and then the sky's the limit!

JB: Everything is a challenge from that point forth.

TB: Yes, but a *meaningful* challenge! That's the reason I enjoyed teaching so much.

JB: That's what young black people need to recognize.

TB: Yes, but I've also taught in schools where all of my students were white, and my message is always the same. I remember one time when the principal of one of those schools decided to put me to the test. You see, in the yearbook for that school, they had a place where they indicated which teacher and which subject the students liked best. Well, about 80 percent of the students said Mr. Black and chose either history or social studies, which were the classes that I had been teaching. Now remember that at that time I am the only black person in that entire school, including the janitors! So some of the white teachers got jealous, and, as a result, one day the principal came into my class unexpectedly to check out what I was doing, and my kids caught the signal and really showed off what they had learned. They really went to town naming and explaining various dates and events. I really didn't have to do anything. They did it all, and so this principal comes over to me and asks me what it is that I think I am teaching. I say, "American history," and he says, "Well, this is not the way we've been teaching it." So I say, "Of course not. This is *corrective* American history," and I ask him if he wants to see my course outline, declaring, "If you doubt any of the things that I have been helping these students find out, then check it out, not by what I say, but by what three hundred respected historians have said, and if what I've been teaching does not jibe with what they have said, then I will alter what I've been teaching, but otherwise I won't."

JB: How did he respond?

TB: Well, he just couldn't handle that. Here was a black man talking to him like another man on an equal basis without any form of compromise and acting as though keeping his job was not the most important thing in the world, which, of course, it isn't.

[*Laughter*]

(*Bridges*, vol. 2, 205–6)

That was not the only principal or school administrator that I had trouble with. But I am proud of the trouble that I caused, and, looking back on all those interviews in *Bridges*, I can honestly say that they were real conversations—I did, and do still, think that way.

In general, I hope my old student Bill Daniels was right, when as a teacher he wrote about me as *his* teacher, sharing some reflections for this volume:

> My approach to teaching was also influenced by Tim Black. I placed students in the center of my teaching, as did Tim Black, who was committed to the total educational experience of his students. I wanted students to step out of the textbooks and into the lives of others. For example, I would bring into my classroom political candidates, governmental officials, and others who were making decisions of value or great significance for our communities. It was important for students to engage in dialogue with persons of leadership and authority, broaden their perspectives, and become more active learners.

Well, I could keep on quoting one interview after another. So many of those I interviewed, in both volumes, are no longer around, and there is a sadness in revisiting their lives. But I am grateful that I was honored to record their stories in this way so that they would not be lost the way so many others have been lost. And past the sadness, over it, these recollections of the way we were do offer some hope and inspiration. There is still a lot to overcome. But we have already overcome a lot, and we need to remember that. We can still do the impossible, maybe even the miraculous. Even when the memories are painful to remember, they are part of the story that we need to remember, the story of that Sacred Ground that made history. And keeps on making it.

CHAPTER 6

The Power and the Glory

As I like to say, I'm retired, but I'm not tired. And that's a good thing, since the last three decades of my life have been busy as ever. For some time now I have been able to say to my audiences, with confidence, "I used to be your age." At ninety-nine, hopefully one hundred years by the time this book appears, I am pretty sure I can say that to all of you reading this book. And all I can say is that I am glad to be here, and that, when I was your age, I did not give up. Sam Cooke used to sing, "Well, you know, I'm so glad. I know the trouble don't last always." And that is still good to keep in mind. I can still hear his voice; I've been singing those words to myself for a long time. And even at my age, and in these times, times that sometimes seem so bad, I can keep on keepin' on, and you can too. I may like my merlot in the evening, but as I told the HistoryMakers, when they asked about my favorite time of day: "I like the sunrise because it brings a new day."

And back at the beginning of the 1990s, just as I was taking on my oral history project, I had no idea how much more history we were about to make. And soon. My friend Carol Elizabeth Moseley Braun, who is a very close friend of my wife Zenobia, was about to become the first black woman to serve as a U.S. senator (and only the second black senator since Reconstruction). She won that seat in 1992 and served until 1999.

Carol was young—she was born in 1947, here on my Sacred Ground, at Forty-First and Indiana—but she had already seen a lot. She was there with the Chicago Freedom Movement in Marquette Park, when Dr. King was hit with that rock. Her approach to nonviolence was like mine—she wanted to throw those rocks back. And she was friendly with the Black Panthers, though she did not go all the way with their views either. She knew the brilliant young Black Panther leader Fred Hampton well, and admired the free breakfast program he launched and the way he was able to get the cooperation of gang leaders, including my old student Jeff Fort. Hampton was one of those brutally murdered in December 1969 by a unit of the state's attorney's office, working with the FBI and the Chicago Police Department. This was part of the same vicious effort, by COINTELPRO, that had been directed against Dr. King. J. Edgar Hoover, the director of the FBI, was terrified of charismatic black leaders such as Fred.

This is not as contradictory as it may sound. Dr. King himself understood very well how the Black Power movement was in some respects like the Black Arts movement—an expression of pride and dignity in being black. It was a way of saying "I am somebody." And sometimes it was hard to tell where the line was between nonviolence as a tactic or strategy and nonviolence as a philosophy or way of life, because Dr. King was so convinced that violence would only backfire and beget more violence. He was obviously religious, and believed that we are all part of one "garment of destiny," as he liked to put it. With those beliefs, he could really believe, deep in his heart, that the universe was on the side of justice. But he did not always talk in those terms. He understood and admired those young leaders, including Malcolm X, despite his differences with them, differences he was always trying to overcome. Had they lived a little longer, King and Malcolm might have been reconciled. We will never know for sure.

Anyway, Carol decided that she was not a revolutionary. Her parents, like my daddy, admired Marcus Garvey and the black nationalism movement. But Carol was independent. She has a lot of integrity. A lot of integrity and a lot of energy. She was one of those who went to a Catholic school—the Catholic schools were often better, and she was a Catholic. She was an extremely well-qualified candidate, and I had already known her for some time before she ran for the Senate. She had been a state representative for many years, winning the IVI-IPO's best legislator award for six years in a row. She won many awards before going to the Senate—from the Chicago Board of Education to the Illinois Women's Caucus, and including awards from gay and lesbian organizations. She was the Cook County recorder of deeds and pushed forward a code of ethics for that organization. She was and is very progressive. She has a law degree from the University of Chicago and became an environmental activist many years ago. She had and has farsighted views on controlling gun violence, improving education, being pro-choice and against the death penalty, and many other crucial issues.

Maybe this is surprising, but her Senate run should have been easier than it was. She had a lot of support, from people like Len Despres as well as Bennett Johnson and myself. But at a certain point, she brought in Kgosie Matthews, one of Jesse Jackson's old operatives, to be her campaign manager, and that turned out to be a problem. He had very little experience and had trouble taking advice, even from those of us who had been around for some time. But some people liked him. My old ally Sam Ackerman thought he was important for moving things ahead. Len and I disagreed, but we had to work together.

Alan Dixon, whose seat Carol was running for, should have been a formidable candidate. He had been in the Senate many years. But he had alienated many of us by voting to confirm Clarence Thomas to the Supreme Court. And as in the case of Harold's election, we were lucky enough to have a third Democratic candidate running in the primary, Albert Hohfeld. He and Dixon split the white vote, and that put Carol through, though it was still close. She went on to defeat the Republican Richard Williamson. She was the first woman senator from Illinois, and the first black woman ever in the Senate. She was the only black senator her entire time in office.

I did not agree with Carol about everything. Sometimes, on economic issues, she was too conservative or centrist. But overall she was a very good senator and a fine person. It was so sad to see her dogged by charges of financial mismanagement, of diverting campaign funds for personal use. Those charges kept coming during her whole time in office. She faced harassment just like Harold did. But she was never convicted of anything; she was never even formally charged with anything. And after she lost her bid for reelection, to the Republican Peter Fitzgerald, she served as the ambassador to New Zealand. And she made some efforts to run for president and for mayor of Chicago, though she has spent much of her time in recent years growing her organic foods and cosmetics businesses.

I cannot help thinking about just how historic it would have been if the first black president of the United States had also been a woman, a woman from my Sacred Ground. Carol could have done it. Could have been, should have been.

Little did I know at the time that I was about to meet the first black president of the United States.

The Power

Barack Obama was a brilliant young man who had just finished law school at Harvard. He was back in Chicago in 1992. He had done some community organizing here before, at Altgeld Gardens in the 1980s, and had trained with some of the Alinskyites, the followers of Saul Alinsky. Then he married Michelle Robinson and got involved with Project Vote, I think through Jackie Grimshaw. Project Vote had a lot of people involved. There was overlap. Jackie had been an active supporter of Harold's, and Obama was in charge of Project Vote when we were trying to get the vote out for Carol, and he raised a lot of money and brought out a lot of votes. He was making friends fast, influential friends like David Axelrod. And Michelle was a true South Sider, good friends with Jesse Jackson's daughter Santita. Obama was already telling his friends that he might run for president someday.

Anyway, it was not too long after he came back to Chicago that he asked to meet with me. We met at the Medici, a long-standing Hyde Park restaurant favored by many of my friends at the university, and he talked to me for hours, asking one question after another about how to build a political base on the South Side. We met a number of times in fact, though I cannot recall too many of the details. I do recall how he struck me right away as very bright. He was a talented young man who was going to be ready when the doors of opportunity swung open. But he had a lot to learn. And I mean a lot.

Here I cannot help but think of the delightful and very relevant interview that I did with Drs. Barbara and James Bowman, who for many years did so much to support and encourage black students at the University of Chicago. They carried on that long legacy of brilliant black doctors on the South Side, going back to Daniel Hale Williams, who performed the first successful heart surgery [pericardium surgery] at Provident Hospital, the black hospital where black doctors and nurses could train. We had a timely conversation about what is now called "code-switching."

BB: Any form of knowledge is very context-specific, and so if you ask me to bring forth my knowledge and apply it in an entirely new situation, it's going to be extremely hard for me. I would have to try a series of different strategies, and sometimes I might just cast around or use trial and error, but whatever I might choose to do, I probably won't seem to be acting at all reasonably because now you have placed things in a new context which I don't quite understand. Let me give you another good example of what I'm talking about. Sylvia Esther Warren talks about the behavior of kids in school. In Appalachia the parents only ask children questions when the parents themselves don't know what the answers are. "Where are those shoes?" "What is your brother doing?" So then, when that child comes to school, the teacher holds up a round, red ball and says to the child, "What is this?" The child doesn't know how to articulate the "correct" response. The child doesn't know because the child hasn't learned how to answer a question like that. Now, of course, the child *knows* that the teacher *knows* what it is that the teacher is holding, and the child also *knows* that the teacher knows that he knows what it is, but then, "Why is she asking me what it is? What does she want me to say?" We've had situations just like that over and over again in Head Start. The teachers would say, "What's your name?" and the child would say, "Robert," and the teacher would interpret this as meaning, "Ah, that poor kid doesn't even know what his last name is." But if you had asked that same child what was his *other* name, he would have told you right away what his last name was. But, in terms of his prior experience, in his neighborhood everybody knew him as "Robert." His family also knew him as "Robert," and for him "Robert" was what you meant when you asked him for his name.

TB: You know, just yesterday I was at our annual Fifty-Eighth Street Picnic. My friends there are very different kinds of guys, and they have their own way of saying things, and so in that kind of situation I guess I had to build a little "bridge" of my own.

BB: Yes, of course, you need to build "bridges" that are very different over there, but someone like you seems to be able to build "bridges" like that in every direction.

TB: But, Barbara, how do you teach someone to build those kind of "bridges" if they don't already know how? For example, my brother tries hard, but he can't build those kind of "bridges." He grew up with the Tilden Tech crowd and the University of Illinois crowd and the Kappa crowd—

BB: And so what he knows, he only knows in that one kind of way.

TB: So when he gets with the Fifty-Eighth Street guys, he is completely out of place. But there are guys just like him, such as Arnie Byrd, who went to the same schools, and yet Arnie is able to fit right in.

BB: Yes, and some people like Jesse Jackson are able to do something that most other people can't do. You can't switch over suddenly to "black" English can you?

TB: Not easily. Sometimes I have to work at it.

BB: Well, Jesse Jackson can talk "black" English and then turn right around and talk "standard" English. Very few people can do that.

TB: And he knows exactly when it is the right time for him to do it.

BB: That's even more important, of course, but the point is that most of us can't do it at all.

TB: King could also do that. He could do it because he was keenly aware of the importance of cultural factors. I heard him preach in his own church, and the way he spoke—

(*Bridges*, vol 1, 597–98)

By the way, the Bowmans were the parents of Valerie Jarrett, a wonderful and extremely talented young lady who of course became good friends with the Obamas and served as the president's senior advisor. She is a charming person who always goes out of her way to ask how this old man is doing whenever we are at some event together.

That was a bit of a digression, but not too much of one. I thought of that conversation with the Bowmans because, when I first met Obama, he could not code-switch to black English at all. Unlike Michelle. People made fun of him for not being black enough, for not being able to talk or walk the right way. He seemed like a bright young man from Harvard, now teaching at the University of Chicago. In his first speeches, even on the South Side, he sounded like a college professor. He was no Harold Washington or Jesse Jackson, and I was impressed but not too optimistic about his future. He did not know much about the black church or its historic role on the South Side. But he fit in pretty well with the Hyde Park liberals, people like Len Despres and Abner Mikva, though even then he was probably more of a centrist than they were.

But Obama learned very quickly. He did a lot of political work, and I recommended him to a lot of old friends like Bill Ayers and Bernardine Dohrn, Michael and Susan Klonsky, Father Pfleger, Jamie Kalven, and many others; they helped him a lot. We were all involved with school reform too, the Small Schools Workshop and other organizations that have done a lot of valuable work to save our Chicago schools. So it was not long before Obama made it to the state senate, where he started getting some very serious advice from seasoned professionals like Emil Jones. His biggest mistake, of course, was to run against Bobby Rush for Rush's seat as congressman for the First Congressional District. That was in 1999. Rush, a former Black Panther who was almost murdered along with Fred Hampton and Mark Clark, beat him by about two to one, and really pushed the case that Barack was not black enough. But I think that many of us, including Bobby, recognized that that was what might make him successful on the national level. Anyway, there was no way that I could support him over Bobby.

But some of us got pretty angry at Obama before that, in 1995. My old friend, the activist Alice Palmer, was exploring a run for the U.S. Congress to replace the scandal-scarred Mel Reynolds. She was going to do that, and not run again for her seat in the Illinois Senate, in 1996. Of course, that was the seat that Barack Obama would win. And at first, Alice even endorsed him. But how he won it was the problem.

When Alice ended up running far behind Jesse Jackson Jr. in the primary, she was ready to give up. But then she decided, and many old friends helped her decide—I was part of the Draft Alice Palmer Committee—to go ahead and seek reelection to her seat in the Illinois Senate, despite her having endorsed Barack. Many of us thought that the right thing to do would be for the younger man to step aside, to defer to someone who was his political senior. We had more faith in Alice Palmer, who was endorsed by the *Defender* and *N'Digo* and had the support of Emil Jones. She was a known quantity and had paid her dues. I was part of the group who confronted Barack, asking him to step down and wait his turn.

Well, he had no intention of doing so. He had done his work and was not about to back out. He had three thousand names on the petition that he filed, and Alice tried in a desperate, last-minute effort to scrape together enough signatures for her petition, but she came up with only about half that and many of them were found to be invalid, as we found out when they were challenged. In Obama's mind, Alice had broken her word to him and then mismanaged her effort to reenter the race. He won easily.

It was not as easy when he won that seat in the U.S. Senate, but luck was on his side. His main rival in the primary, Blair Hull, had to drop out when confronted with allegations of domestic abuse. His Republican rival in the election, Jack Ryan, also had to quit, because of the sex scandals that emerged. The Republicans did not know what to do, so they found a black conservative, Alan Keyes, but Keyes was so crazy that he actually seemed to help Obama. Keyes made even Clarence Thomas look good. It was a landslide, with Obama winning 70 percent of the vote. He was not in the Senate long, and as they say, the rest is history.

Looking back on it, I still feel some anger, a little anger, that Obama was so quick to ignore the advice of his elders, the advice that he had sought out. But he is a politician, an undeniably talented politician, and politicans always remind me of my grandma's comment—"Baby, I cain't hear whatcha sayin' because whatcha doin' talks so loud." This was hardly the only time that my advice was ignored. Still, when he decided to run for the presidency, he had my full support. I could not understand why some of my old friends would still carry those grudges instead of uniting behind this remarkable young man. He was not at all perfect, but he was historic.

I went to the inauguration and it was a great day, a day I never dreamed I would see, as magical as the March on Washington. Now I felt that the miraculous really had happened. The young president had a very difficult road ahead of him, with the economic situation and all. But I had lived through the Depression, and I knew those hard times would pass. And now, instead of FDR, we had a black president, someone who, although not originally from the South Side, could only have reached those heights via the South Side, through my Sacred Ground. I could not help but feel that pride.

I was back in Washington in September of 2016, the final days of Obama's presidency, for the opening of the long-awaited National Museum of African American History and Culture, thanks to my old friend Lonnie Bunch. I could not help thinking about how historic it was that this event was happening under Obama's presidency. I felt that same pride. And then there was the opening of the King Memorial in 2011. People should not underestimate the significance of these great developments; whatever the actions of the current occupant of the White House, the face of history has changed and every tourist in Washington will see that firsthand.

Of course, once Obama made it to the White House, it was hard to get past his handlers and gatekeepers. It was the same situation that I saw with Harold, when someone you have helped gets too distant from his roots, sometimes realizing it, sometimes not. So much happened to him, so quickly—becoming president, winning the Nobel Peace Prize, and all that. He had a lot to be thinking about. But I took special pride in this president for being free of all forms of scandal and setting such a good example for all the young people in this country—for all people everywhere. If he was not always as progressive as I would have liked, he was always at least bending that way and a very decent man, and you had to be kind of crazy not to see that. Sadly, as we saw, many people in this country had a lot of trouble accepting a black president, and at times it seemed to me like we were seeing on the national level the same kind of racist obstruction that Harold had confronted when he won office.

I was moved practically to tears when, soon after Obama had won, I received a handwritten note from him on my ninetieth birthday. It was read aloud at my birthday party:

> I wish I could be with you all in person today to celebrate the life
> of a dedicated teacher and one of the preeminent oral historians

of our time, a man who keeps the soul of the South Side alive and shares his stories still, Professor Tim Black.

The Great Migration brought his family to Chicago's South Side, and the Great Depression started him down the long path of social justice. As a student at Burke Elementary School, he'd often walk across the street to hear the orators in Washington Park argue with passion for jobs that pay a fair wage, for protections to keep workers safe, for an economy that would allow families to live in dignity and dream of a brighter future. Little did they know among their greatest lasting impacts would be the achievements of the man we honor today.

Like my grandfather, he joined the army as a fresh-faced young man in World War II. And like my great uncle, he helped liberate the Buchenwald concentration camp. It was a moment that left a mark on this man; that left no doubt as to his destiny. He returned convinced by his life experiences that the greatest impact he could make on the next generation would be to teach our youth about their communities, about the world they live in, and about how to be responsible citizens of each.

For forty years, he shaped our young men and women into those citizens. And though he may have retired from the teaching profession nearly two decades ago, he never stopped being a teacher. We are all his students in a classroom that never closes. Because of Professor Black, jazz has a place to call home in Chicago. Because of Professor Black, the rich and vibrant chronicles of Bronzeville and the greater South Side live on. Because of Professor Black, generations of youth have grown up with a better appreciation of their neighborhoods and the history they inherit.

The man we honor today grew up in the midst of Depression and war, yet considers himself part of a fortunate generation. And he's made it his life's mission to give each successive generation every possible chance in this world. "I never lose hope," he once said. "I believe that I have responsibilities to help younger people to obtain hopes and dreams. Their present condition may be very discouraging; my aim is to help them regain a sense of hope for the future. My main interest is in building a better America, building a better world."

Tim, for your birthday, I promise you this: that will always be my mission too. Thank you for a life well-lived. I wish you all the best for the stories you've yet to tell.

Happy Birthday,
Barack Obama

I believe that he is still trying to keep that promise, with the Obama Presidential Center, even though he is no longer in office. But I will say more about that a little later on.

Now, I was not exactly quiet during the Obama presidency. He had many critics on the Left, from Cornel West to Jesse Jackson to Mike Pfleger, and their arguments were often the ones that I could most sympathize with. I started writing regular columns for the *Hyde Park Herald* and the *Lakefront Outlook*, and those gave me the opportunity to make my views known. I think that one column that I wrote toward the end of Obama's time in office does a decent job of summing up my perspective on his presidency, so I would like to share it here:

President Barack Obama has proven to African Americans, other minorities, males, females and other groups and the world that in America we can do the impossible. Who would have thought 20 years ago or less than that, that an African American would be the president of the United States of America?

Obama was prepared to be the President as others had been. The opportunity was there, and his personality created a base of support and appreciation that made it possible for him to become the first African-American President in the history of the United States.

I think a part of Obama's legacy is that it will encourage younger people of all races, gender and ethnic groups to see that the impossible can be possible, and that one has to be prepared when the door has been opened for the opportunity.

His healthcare plan, the Affordable Care Act also known as ObamaCare, is also a part of that legacy, Medicaid and the expansion of Medicare, so that it now gives almost every American an opportunity to have healthcare, which was not possible before.

I think his foreign policy and relationships, though contradictory, have helped to bring more of our allies closer together with part of the leadership of the United States of America.

I think his attitude on climate change and his attempts to bring more support have been the kinds of things that are universal and will continue to be appreciated by not just Americans but by people in other parts of the world.

In the Middle East, bringing people together against ISIS has been helpful to our allies in that part of the world. I think it has brought confidence to those nations and that they now have support outside of their own territories.

The Obamas in the White House have been tremendous. He has not been as perfect for many younger African Americans as they thought he ought to be but what they may not realize is that he had to make compromises. Of course it's easy to understand that if Obama were not a black man some of that legislation would have probably gone through fairly easy.

Since he and his wife Michelle spent a great deal of their developing lives in Hyde Park, I think it has been an inspiration as well as an example of how Hyde Park has made a difference in the lives of many politicians including the late Harold Washington, Carol Moseley Braun, and others.

Since World War II Hyde Park has been a very liberal and inclusive community along racial and ethnic lines. Many of these people who supported and became allies of Barack Obama such as David Axelrod and Valerie Jarrett were Hyde Parkers and have been close to him before he became President and since he became President.

Hyde Parkers should feel a sense of pride and should be prideful that Obama chose the Hyde Park/Jackson Park area for his Presidential library where his political life began.

For me having lived as long as I have lived and seen the emergence of very conservative forces in Europe, Germany, and Italy and in other places I have a sense of comparison as President-Elect Donald Trump takes office.

He said he will "Make America Great Again." The old, "great" America that he is talking about does not include an opportunity for all Americans and peace and justice in our relationships with our foreign allies.

We have lost a good deal of the progress, which Barack Obama has made possible by continuing the legacy of Dr. Martin Luther King and the Civil Rights movement.

The fears that young people have about Trump's plans for immigration reform, bringing back stop-and frisk policing, repealing the Affordable Care Act and some of his other agenda items are justified. I am very proud of young people for having those feelings because I believe that young people with the experiences of their older relatives and friends will not allow Trump another opportunity to destroy this country.

I know that we will overcome Trump's ideas of a "great" America because I have inspiration that was given to me by the success by Barack and Michelle Obama.

I think my words are still relevant today, as we watch the person in the White House destroying the dignity and sanity that the Obamas represented. Where is the voice of the people, of those many Americans, a majority, who want peace and justice, decent medical care, Social Security, and a living wage? Fortunately, it will not go unheard for long. In all the days of my years, I have never witnessed anything quite like the #MeToo movement, and I am optimistic that maybe it represents a new day in our politics, one that is long overdue. I supported Hillary Clinton for president mainly because it is time we had a woman president. I believe we soon will.

Yes, Black Lives Matter

But at this point, I would like to say something in a different tone, something about some of the issues that troubled me the most under Obama's presidency, and that trouble me still. These are issues that I cannot think about without feeling anger and agitation.

In February 2012, George Zimmerman murdered young Trayvon Martin in cold blood. There have been many such racist killings, including many since, but this one struck a nerve and became the catalyst for a national movement which endures to this day, years later. Many people have asked me what I think about the Black Lives Matter movement, and I tell them: *This is the continuation of our struggle*. There are forces who seek to erase us. I am proud of our young people for standing up.

People referred and continue to refer to him simply as "Trayvon." As if we knew him personally. We identify so closely with him and with his parents, who displayed great dignity throughout the trial of his murderer, Zimmerman. We think of Trayvon as a beloved young son of the entire African American people.

Around our kitchen tables, it's the topic of serious discussion. Within our families, we have the full gamut of emotions, confusions, and attitudes about the murder of Trayvon Martin and the many others who have fallen victim to such violence. Families express fear especially for their sons. We want to be firm and steadfast in the face of racist violence. But we don't want our children to act rashly or become victims. Many place our hope for the future in the name of the Lord, or in our belief in the law and its processes.

The overwhelming emotional responses of African Americans and others have been deep disappointment, grief, and anger. But not despair. The outpouring of protestors in Chicago, in New York and L.A. and San Francisco and Baltimore, shows that people want to get organized and act powerfully.

When people ask me what we ought to do in this situation, I think it's already beginning to happen: on a practical level we have to organize more demonstrations and visit our public officials in the states where we *can* still vote and tell them in no uncertain terms that if they don't take action their political careers will be brief.

What gets my goat is hearing the reporters and the jurists who said that race was not a factor in the jury's deliberations, in this case and in others. I bet most people anywhere in the world would agree that race was and remains a motivating factor. If Trayvon had been white, that man would probably not have shot him. Conversely, if Trayvon had been the shooter, he'd be going to prison for life—at best. In Florida, he'd get the death penalty. They may not have much down there, but they still have the electric chair. Don't tell me race is not a factor. That verdict should have put an end to talk of a "postracial America," and if it didn't I don't know what will. The Obamas represented all that I have said, but no one should take that to mean that we are now in a postracial society. You can just look at the violent reaction to Obama himself.

Those of us who are old enough to remember—we've seen this all before—might be reminded of the trial of the Scottsboro Boys, who were framed up for rape in the early 1930s in my family's home state of Alabama. I'm thinking too of the murder of Emmett Till in Mississippi in the mid-1950s. At the trials, the message was the same eighty years ago, and sixty years ago: "He was up to no good." "They were up to something." Racial profiling is nothing new, and it provides the same sorry excuse to do violence to black men now as it did then.

But both the Scottsboro frame-up and the Emmett Till murder were met by massive organizing campaigns by the freedom movement. We made sure that people understood that both legal lynching and literal lynching were motivated by racial hatred, not "self-defense." We organized about these cases, sometimes years before we had yet heard of Dr. King.

The trial of the accused murderers of Emmett Till was for many Americans, and especially for black Americans, a moment of revelation. They witnessed how the carefully constructed defense case exonerated those Klansmen. The trial and the not-guilty verdict elevated our political consciousness. The entire black community, whether rich or poor, articulate or uneducated, knew what had happened. Less than six months after Emmett Till's murder, the Montgomery bus boycott began, and the mass movement took on a national scale and began to gather international attention.

It would be roughly another decade before the Voting Rights Act became the law of the land. And even then, it was to be subject to renewal by Congress every ten years. In 2013 these Dixie Republicans were able to go before the U.S. Supreme Court—after half a century—and argue with a straight face, "We no longer need all these restrictions on voting regulations. We don't need them anymore." And the conservatives on the court—including a black man who wouldn't even be there, save for the victories of the civil rights movement—removed the heart of the Voting Rights Act. It will enable the states to resurrect so-called regulations and tests that can eliminate poor folks from the voting rolls, and most of them will be black, which is how things were before.

People ask me how it makes me feel, to see the reversal of so much progress. Does it feel like my life's work is being undone? My answer: *I am aggravated, but not discouraged.*

Why? Because we *have* seen what the power of an awakened people can accomplish. If anything, I am even more firm in my determination to continue, not to stop. I am not surprised at all by this turn of events. It's all part of life in a society dominated by a powerful, conservative, money-hungry class of people who are less than 2 percent of the population.

Somebody asked me: If you could sit down with Clarence Thomas and talk sense to him, what would you say to him? I responded that I don't think Clarence Thomas can be talked to. He does not care for the opinions or pleas of black people.

What we need to do now is *not* to try to win over one or another of these conservatives. We need to secure an amendment that once again takes those voting restrictions out of order, that restores the principle of our Constitution that all men and women are created equal. In the South—and elsewhere—they will place new obstacles in the paths of those who want to cast a vote. We need to press Congress to put teeth back into the Voting Rights Act. We will need to fight gerrymandering in the courts and on the street. I remember my father went to vote in Alabama, and one of the questions they would pose was, "Did your grandfather vote?" My father's grandfather, of course, was a slave. This was used to try to deny him the right to vote. Others, even highly educated blacks in Alabama, were given tasks like answering a question written in French or in German. All sorts of stunts to knock them out of the voting place. And this is the sort of thing they want to reintroduce, in order to limit the right to vote.

I first voted when I was twenty-one, long before the age was lowered to eighteen. At that time, back in the late 1930s, your parents expected you to register and to vote. In Chicago, the black population often voted in far greater percentage than all other groups, including immigrant and ethnic groups. Perhaps we had a greater appreciation of voting because we had been so long denied this right in the South. Even during World War II, we voted while in combat. We didn't give up the franchise. We had fought too hard to get it. When young people now ask me, "Why should I bother to vote?" I say to them, "Someone is going to be in that office; it will either be X or Y. Which one do you want to see there?"

I should also admit that in Chicago we are dealing with another sort of autocratic government. In spite of the express wishes of tens of thousands of Chicagoans, we have a local government that is trampling on the black community and its institutions, especially its schools. We need to improve our democratic practices right here in Chicago. We need the energy and the knowledge to speak and stand up. We need to confront the legislators at our local and state level, particularly those who have some control of the money, such as those on the finance committees, so that they hear our demands and consider their political futures.

They ignore us at their peril. All our recent mayors were elected because of the black vote—Jane Byrne, Harold Washington, Richard M. Daley, and now Rahm Emanuel. But black registration is now way down. We've got to organize. You know, while he was in the U.S. Congress, Harold Washington—before he became mayor—was the lead person on the extension of the Voting Rights Act. He understood the power that it represented. Let's talk to our young people about this history, and let's talk about the importance of retaining and extending real democracy. How will your life be affected if the Voting Rights Act is not enforced in its original spirit and intent? Our young people's futures will be profoundly diminished. But it's not too late. It's not irreversible.

Let's make sure we are out there pressing the demands for justice in the spirit of the marchers and martyrs who fought for equality in 1963, and in memory of our sons Emmett Till and Trayvon Martin.

As the saying goes, freedom is a constant struggle. This is no time to slack off. It's time to organize and fight back. We won justice before, and we can win it again. I look back and I recall how the murder of Emmett Till and the subsequent horror, rage, and anguish forged the modern civil rights movement. Mamie Till, the grieving mother, insisted that the public not be spared the viewing of the carnage which had been done to her child's body. The casket was opened and the ravaged remains of Emmett Till were photographed, and tens of thousands of people viewed the horrific sight as they paid their last respects.

It seems that no one walked away unmoved. Moved not only to pain and sorrow at the sight of such suffering, but moved to become part of a great movement. Today I am so heartened when I hear our young people who are similarly outraged and moved to act and to organize, fighting against the police violence, gun violence, violence in schools and against women, and more. We see them protesting in New York City, in Baltimore, in Chicago, in St. Louis—in so many cities and towns where young black men and women have been subject to racist violence including unwarranted police violence.

Today, sadly, we can all recite a longer list of names of those victims. Laquan McDonald, Tamir Rice, Mike Brown, Eric Garner, Tony Robinson, Rekia Boyd, Freddie Gray, and so many more, from all over the country. But young people have taken the lead on campuses and communities in declaring Black Lives Matter. It makes me proud and confident when I hear them speak. They have analyzed the situation. They insist that the death of an unarmed black young person is not to be diminished. Every life matters, of course, but it is the black youths who feel targeted, disregarded, and unrecognized. Yes, Black Lives Matter. Hell, yes. Black lives have value. Whether they are alive or long gone, our lives have meaning and value. The lives of slaves had value. The lives of our young people today have value. Isn't it part of the same story?

This has been a bit heated, but even at my age my anger can still be strong. Still, as Dr. King showed, anger is not enough, anger needs to go somewhere, needs to go from destruction to construction. We need to channel our anger in a way that makes for positive change. The change has to come, and the question is always: How are we going to get there?

The Glory

Now all during these years, I have still been working on my oral histories—the third volume has yet to appear, but I hope it will—and in what seemed to be a mood of balance between nostalgia for the past and hope for the future. So many of the interviews in *Bridges* had, beneath the surface, an elegiac tone, a lament for a world that was gone. Or at least rapidly disappearing. There have been so many funerals. It seems that every week I am saying goodbye to one of those bridges of memory. Sometimes, it seemed, to the whole community. In my interview with Charles Mingo, who became principal of DuSable High School, we were talking about the neighborhood and the Robert Taylor Homes housing project, which at that time, in 1992, was still right across State Street. He thought the whole idea of the Taylor Homes was a mistake, and then I asked him about the neighborhood:

> **TB:** At the present time, as you were saying, there is almost nothing outside of this building that is available to youngsters. After you have restructured Taylor, and reorganized the neighborhood, what would you bring into the neighborhood of a recreational or entertainment nature?

> **CM:** I would reopen the Met Theater. I would even go and take the auditorium of DuSable High School and open it up as a theater

on the weekends. I would stimulate small businesses in the area. People who have money can purchase services, and if we had full employment for the parents, then there would be cleaners and other services that people could use. Someone could own a grocery store. Someone could own some other kinds of stores and provide other kinds of services. But, you see, when you have a poverty community, all of the strength of the neighborhood moves out, and then you have nonresident people who have no interests in the community coming in and providing all the service. Just try and find a first-rate supermarket between Twenty-Second and Fifty-Fifth Streets!

TB: And there are no movie houses at all!

CM: That's right. The closest movie house you can go to would be at Evergreen Plaza or downtown or maybe the Hyde Park Theater, but they don't want people from our community over there in places like that, and they make that perfectly clear!

TB: So our youngsters have to go out of their neighborhood just to have a good time, and when they do, it often becomes a form of social embarrassment for them and their friends.

CM: It's more than just an embarrassment. It's much worse than that, and all because places such as the Evergreen Plaza have a theater, and we don't have one of our own down here anymore.

TB: When you were still a young man, I would imagine that the ma-and-pa kinds of businesses and various recreational facilities also afforded some opportunities for young people to get jobs.

CM: That's right. You could always find work at the places like that. As a matter of fact, my brothers and I, we grew up around the Court Theater at Fifty-Third and Wentworth, affectionately known as the dump, and you could always get a summer job there working as an usher or something.

TB: And when there were small ma-and-pa grocery stores, you could also always get a job as a delivery boy. That's the way that communities are built and maintained.

CM: Right, and at one point I worked in the Wentworth Supermarket on Calumet, but now those stores that you do have here are hiring people who do not look like the people who come into those stores to shop. That's not the way things should be. So what I am basically advocating is that we tear down a third of each one of those project buildings and then build some parking lots and some recreational areas, even some tennis courts and things like that. But the most important thing is to give these folks some jobs so they can earn some money and be able to rebuild their neighborhood and turn things around.

(*Bridges*, vol. 2, 358–59)

But somehow, deep as my love is for the history of my Sacred Ground, I find it hard to sustain that tone. I'm still not depressed. I might be angry, I might be aggravated, I might be all sorts of things, but I am still not depressed. One of the best parts of Obama's success, for me and many others, was the way in which it made the South Side of Chicago again seem like the center of the black universe. And in the last two decades, this old hoodlum has been able to glory in this new renaissance.

Now, if you live long enough, you have a birthday party or get some recognition now and then. I've been fortunate in that respect. I've received some awards—whether I deserved them or not, I cannot say. My generation of civil rights leaders is gradually disappearing from the scene, and as one of the last ones standing, I probably get more than my fair share of recognition just for still being here.

For sixty years I taught and wrote on many topics, but I had left my doctoral studies in order to plunge fully into the civil rights movement, so I had remained "ABD." I had completed all the required coursework for my doctorate, but I left without writing my doctoral dissertation. The pull of the movement was too strong. Over six decades I did not allow myself to be called "Doctor," because I didn't have that Ph.D. and I didn't want to misrepresent my attainment. Thus it was a special pleasure to return to Roosevelt University in 2008 to be awarded an honorary Doctorate of Humane Letters. I am now a Dr., as well as a Prof. I only wish that my mama had been able to brag about that.

Among the many celebrations, the recognition by the University of Chicago has been meaningful to me. I have had a complicated relationship with the university—part of that American conundrum that I keep talking about. When I first applied to the graduate program in social sciences back in the early 1950s, an administrator told me I had come to the wrong place. There were few black graduate students, and black students with families lived in separate, segregated university housing facilities.

Fortunately, through lots of struggle and social ferment, the university has changed with the times. Let us not forget that before running for political office at the state level, Barack Obama himself was a member of the law school faculty. There is still a lot of change that needs to happen, but developments like the new level one trauma center, which came about through the power of community protest, show that important change can happen and make a difference.

In particular, the university's Civic Knowledge Project, or CKP, has meant a lot to me. This organization started working with me back around 2003, and our collaboration has led to a great deal of recognition on the part of the university. Thanks to people who knew about me through the Civic Knowledge Project, especially the historians Leora Auslander and Tom Holt, I was nominated for, and won in 2012, one of the university's highest honors, the Benton Medal for Distinguished Public Service. This award "recognizes persons who have rendered distinguished public service in the field of education," and I was honored with a panel discussion featuring some very distinguished speakers, some of those brilliant young scholars whose work I admire so much.

After I received the Benton Medal, the university launched an annual series called the Timuel D. Black Bridges of Memory Distinguished Guest Lecture and Jazz Concert. The first venue was the legendary Parkway Ballroom at Forty-Fourth and King Drive. The Parkway was a landmark in the big band era. I was there the night the Parkway Ballroom opened in 1940, back when you had to dress up in your black tie and tails to walk in there. Duke Ellington was up there playing. We walked up that curving staircase, and we said to each other, "Look what these n——s have built!" It was shiny and new, the most elegant spot in town. It was wonderful to be back there after all those years.

Of course, back in those years I earned my living selling insurance, burial policies mostly, out of the Metropolitan, the black-owned insurance company which occupied the first floor of the building, with the Parkway Ballroom up above. It had a huge kitchen and a café in the back upstairs, where we often ate lunch while working for the Metropolitan. In the late 1960s the Parkway went into decline and for a long time was unused. A local developer bought and rehabilitated the building, and it has once again become a center for cultural activities, private parties, and celebrations in the community.

The inaugural lecture was delivered by Kenneth Warren, professor in the English department of the University of Chicago, and author of many works on African American literature. His lecture was followed by a classic jazz performance by the Ari Brown Band. For me this was the ideal combination: the scholarly analysis and reflection by Professor Warren, followed by my favorite music. Since then the lecture series has continued, highlighting the work of scholars and spreading the joy and nostalgia of great jazz. To see all those people, hundreds of them, both young and old, enjoying both scholarship and the music that means so much to me—well, that can confirm your faith in the power of education and the power of music.

The lecture series has been created and directed by my friend and colleague Bart Schultz, the philosopher who leads the Civic Knowledge Project. The Civic Knowledge Project is an exemplary program. It not only enriches the knowledge of the relationships with the communities around the University of Chicago, but also inspires the building of community between the academic life of the university and its neighboring communities. There is a sharing of the life of both, and that is progress.

In retirement, the Civic Knowledge Project has kept me exceptionally busy with writing and speaking and talking with community groups, classes, and young researchers. And then there's my "career" as a tour guide. For more than ten years. I've been leading tours and short courses about the history of Chicago's South Side. These have been organized primarily by Bart and the Civic Knowledge Project, which strives to orient students to the community that surrounds the campus. Too often, Bart felt, students were led to think that the leafy campus of the university was surrounded by a dangerous slum with nothing to offer and from which nothing might be learned. Now, when new college students arrive at UChicago, they get the opportunity to talk to this elder and learn a little bit about their new home. I still love talking with young people.

Giving these bus tours and walking tours has offered students and others the opportunity to learn about Chicago's South Side. These tours and courses have not only helped me recall events from my ninety-nine years on Chicago's South Side, but have also, I hope, helped the participants to understand what St. Clair Drake famously called the "Black

Metropolis" and what I call Sacred Ground—to understand that the seg-regated black communities in Chicago were home to many historically outstanding and influential people in the areas of economics, politics, culture, and social relationships.

There are many places still existing, such as the DuSable Museum, founded by nationally known artists and social activists such as my friend Margaret Burroughs. During these tours, we have a chance to visit the DuSable Museum and other sites associated with Margaret, including the South Side Community Art Center, which she also helped to found. This art center was officially opened by then First Lady Eleanor Roos-evelt in 1940, and remains open today providing free studio art classes and exhibitions. We visit sites where artists and writers—Langston Hughes, Richard Wright, Gwendolyn Brooks—practiced their craft, like the Cleveland Hall Branch Library, an architectural gem.

On our tours, we pass such places as the mansion of Robert Abbott, founder of the *Defender*, which sits by what was then called Grand Bou-levard, then South Park, and now Martin Luther King Drive. I also talk about the old South Center department store and the old Regal Theater, where many young people such as myself had the opportunity to see and hear great musical artists like Duke Ellington, Cab Calloway, and many others.

We might head north, past the famous Eighth Regimental Armory and up to the Wabash Avenue YMCA, where in 1926 Carter G. Wood-son founded Negro History Week, now known as Black History Month. I was very young at the time, but I was there, with my daddy.

Moving along, we pass the sites of former bars and clubs, such as the Sunset Café and Grand Terrace, where Louis Armstrong and many oth-ers popularized jazz and city blues. One time we even had some musicians re-create the "Calling the Children Home" trumpet battles that Arm-strong would have with King Oliver, when they were competing to get customers to come to their clubs on opposite sides of the streets. We just took over the street and listened to the music. Moving north up State Street, we pass the building where Anthony Overton created not only his famous cosmetics company, but also the Douglass National Bank, and we also talk about Jesse Binga and the Binga Bank. There is the old Chicago Bee building, and other sites associated with the many African American businesses that were created in historic Bronzeville. We might meet up with John Lewis, the son of Julian Herman Lewis and Anthony

Overton's daughter Eva, who still lives in the neighborhood. The Civic Knowledge Project cohosted a conference celebrating his father, the first black to join the faculty of the University of Chicago, back in 1917.

Sometimes, with our Dr. Martin Luther King Legacy tours, we visit Liberty Baptist Church, Dr. King's organizing headquarters on Chicago's South Side. And the RainbowPUSH Coalition, for a conversation with the brilliant and still very active Rev. Jesse Jackson Sr., or the Faith Community of St. Sabina, where the fearless and charismatic Rev. Father Michael Pfleger is doing such great work, also carrying on Dr. King's legacy. Then we might go out to the West Side, to North Lawndale to visit the Dr. Martin Luther King Jr. Fair Housing Exhibition Center, built on the site where Dr. King lived during his time in Chicago in 1966. We have also visited Marquette Park, as noted the site of one of the most violent attacks on Dr. King and the civil rights marchers (again, I was there). During these tours and courses, I often recall my work with Dr. King, such as my part in organizing the March on Washington. But we also engage the participants with these powerful examples of how to carry Dr. King's legacy forward. That was also the message on April 4, 2018, when Bart interviewed me in front of eight hundred people at Rockefeller Chapel to commemorate the fiftieth anniversary of Dr. King's tragic assassination. Even today, now more than fifty years after his death, Dr. King can help us channel that anger into something positive, the construction of a better world. At Rockefeller, I recalled how angry I was when I first heard that Dr. King had been assassinated. I was at the hospital visiting my daddy, who was dying, and was in the elevator with two white policemen, who were disparaging Dr. King and the civil rights movement. I turned to them and said, "I wish it was you." But I knew then, as I know now, that the anger was not enough, that it needed to be channeled the way Dr. King channeled it, and turned into action for social justice.

I am glad to help University of Chicago students and other participants to understand the importance of black life in Chicago, from the first Great Migration through the second Great Migration and down to the present day. This contributes in important ways to community life, enriches the knowledge of African American life during these periods, and demonstrates too why the Obama Presidential Center had to be situated on Chicago's South Side. In doing these tours, talks, and workshops, I often find myself looking forward even while I am looking backward. The memories do crowd the corners of my mind, but they leave plenty of room for thinking about the future.

In 2013, the city honored me with its first Champion of Freedom Award, and I was given an honorary street, a stretch of State Street right alongside my old school DuSable. When we go by there and I look up at that sign, I think what my old gang would say if they saw that. And there is now even a garden in my honor on the University of Chicago campus, the Timuel D. Black Edible Arts Garden, located at 5710 South Woodlawn, at the Center for Identity and Inclusion. Bart built that, and we had a gala opening there, with Zenobia and Carol and so many old friends and students. And more honors from the university have come to me—such as the Diversity Leadership Award, in 2015.

So, I have a lot to be grateful for, and I do appreciate the efforts of the many nonprofits and political organizations that have given me some recognition. I hope these events have helped them to build up their members' knowledge and to build support for the work of such organizations as the Chicago Urban League, the IVI-IPO, the Chicago Public Library Foundation, and others that have chosen to recognize me in my later years. I am so glad that my archive—the work of all those years—is now part of the Harsh Collection at the Carter G. Woodson Branch Library, formally the Chicago Public Library, Carter G. Woodson Regional Library, Vivian G. Harsh Research Collection of Afro-American History and Literature. It is a resource for all the young scholars to come, and I hope they make good use of it. There is a lot, too much, that I can no longer remember, and again I apologize to all those who have been part of my life but are not part of this book. Maybe those young scholars will be able to do you the justice you deserve and straighten out some of the things that I might be getting wrong, even if this is the way I remember it. There is even a Timuel D. Black Fund, organized by the Vivian G. Harsh Society, which provides fellowships to young scholars in African American studies. There are many, many good causes—important new causes too, like environmental justice—but I hope you will forgive this old man for thinking that education and jazz deserve your support.

Anyway, I am so grateful to all of these institutions and individuals for their support. All I can say to all of them is a sincere thank you.

Of course I hear from lots of politicians these days. It often seems that everyone running for office wants a photo op with me, wants to get that picture to make it look like we are friends and I am supporting them. I know when it is election time, even without checking the calendar. But I still go my own way. I support my old friends and colleagues, people like Chuy García, but I have to keep speaking up and speaking out about the problems I see.

Still, I have to admit that I was honored and moved when my old friend Senator Richard Durbin introduced, in October 2017, the following tribute in the Congressional Record:

TRIBUTE TO TIMUEL D. BLACK, JR.

Mr. DURBIN. Mr. President, sometimes, when I am asked to describe my politics, I say, "I believe in the Gospel of Saints Paul"—Paul the Apostle, Paul Douglas, Paul Simon, and Paul Wellstone.

Paul the Apostle was, of course, one of the most important figures in the history of the early Christian Church. Paul Douglas, Paul Simon, and Paul Wellstone were Members of this Senate and champions of human rights and human dignity.

This Friday, another champion of human rights and human dignity—Dr. Timuel Black—will honored [sic] by Citizen Action Illinois with its ninth annual Pauls Award, named for Paul Simon and Paul Wellstone.

I am lucky enough to have been friends with both Pauls— Simon and Wellstone. I am sure that they would have approved heartily of the decision to honor Dr. Black with an award bearing their names.

Dr. Timuel Black is a decorated World War II veteran, an educator, author, labor leader, civil rights activist, and historian—and a bender of the moral arc of the universe. He is a visionary and— for me and so many others—a personal hero.

Timuel Black was born in 1918, in Birmingham, AL—the son of a sharecropper and the grandson of slaves.

He was 8 months old when his family moved to Chicago—the first wave of the great migration of African Americans from the Deep South to the North. They settled in a part of town called the Black Belt, now known as Bronzeville.

He attended DuSable High School, a legendary all-Black public high school, where his classmates included Nat King Cole and John Johnson, who would go on to found *Jet* and *Ebony* magazines.

On his 23rd birthday, Japan bombed U.S. Navy ships at Pearl Harbor.

He served 2 years in a segregated U.S. Army. He participated in the Battle of the Bulge, the invasion of Normandy and the liberation of Paris, and he earned four battle stars.

He thought he had seen the worst of World War II—then he witnessed what had happened at Buchenwald, the Nazi concentration camp.

The horrors that he witnessed at that death camp changed his life.

For a time, he was filled with despair. Then he resolved to spend the rest of his life doing whatever he could to advance the causes of human rights and human dignity.

He returned to Chicago and earned an undergraduate degree from Roosevelt University and a master's degree from the University of Chicago.

He helped establish the Congress of Racial Equality. He also helped found a labor union that helped me work my way through college: the United Packinghouse Workers of America.

He began his professional career as a social worker, but he quickly discovered that his real love was "teaching young men and women about the world they live in and how to be responsible citizens of that world."

He spent more than 40 years as a teacher, including positions at DuSable and other Chicago public schools, as well as Roosevelt University, Columbia College Chicago and schools in the City Colleges of Chicago system.

Timuel Black was watching television in December 1955 when he saw "this good-looking man in Montgomery, Alabama." He was so moved that he boarded a plane to meet him.

A year later, Tim Black convinced that young man to come to Chicago—the first time Dr. Martin Luther King would speak in the city.

In 1963, Dr. Black helped organize the Freedom Trains that carried thousands of Chicagoans to hear Dr. King and others speak at the foot of the Lincoln Memorial in Washington, DC. He was there when Dr. King delivered his immortal "I Have a Dream" speech.

He was with Dr. King in 1966 when an angry mob jeered him in Chicago's Marquette Park neighborhood.

In 1983, Tim Black provided influential support to help elect another of his DuSable High School classmates, Harold Washington, the first African-American mayor of Chicago.

Some years later, a young community organizer who had just returned to Chicago with a Harvard law degree asked Professor Black to teach him about organizing people so they could create a better life for themselves and their children.

Over the years, Professor Black and that young organizer became good friends.

On January 20, 2009, it was my privilege to invite Professor Black and his incredible wife, Zenobia Johnson-Black, to be my guests as that community organizer swore an oath to become President of the United States of America—Barack Obama.

My friend, Paul Wellstone, had a beautiful definition of politics. He used to say: In the last analysis, politics is not predictions and politics is not observations. Politics is what we do. Politics is what we do, politics is what we create, by what we work for, by what we hope for and what we dare to imagine.

Dr. Timuel Black has witnessed injustice and inhumanity, but he has never stopped working to believe in a better world, and he has never stopped working to make that world a reality. He is a true inspiration, a Chicago treasure, and an American hero.

I guess my story can't be all wrong, since it is a matter of record, though as for being an inspiration, treasure, and hero, those words belong to the Sacred Ground that this book has tried to describe, all the families and friends, people and places, elders and ancestors, communities and conundrums. My life has been only a reflection—and only a limited, partial reflection—of that bigger historical movement and moment. Each of us is a somebody, and a story, one worth listening to. But all of us are only parts of something much bigger, and for me, that spiritual story of this Sacred Ground is the most important story.

I should add one more thing here. There was one big development in recent years that had my very enthusiastic support—bringing Obama's library to Chicago, specifically to the South Side of Chicago. The Obama Presidential Center, as it is now called, clearly belonged here. Everything I have said in this book shows how this is the Sacred Ground that carries so much black history, including black political history. Obama could not have succeeded from anywhere else. He admits that and likes to say that Chicago's South Side was what brought the pieces of his life together. But he was riding on the tide of all those who had gone before—from Oscar De Priest to Jesse Jackson to Harold Washington to Carol Moseley Braun. He only came to Chicago because he was inspired by the example of Harold. Although sometimes he might be a little forgetful about it, he is a product of this Sacred Ground, and he needs to honor his debt to it, just like me.

I never thought there was any question or doubt about where the Obama library belonged. I was glad when the University of Chicago and the city got together and really pushed the project forward. I was a member of the Community Advisory Committee, along with people like Carol Adams, who became CEO of the DuSable Museum, and Pastor Byron Brazier, the son of the Bishop Brazier I interviewed for *Bridges*, who took over the Apostolic Church of God after his father. I wrote columns, editorials, and letters to the editor, and spoke at one community forum after another. Of course, I wanted the library to be over by Washington Park, closer to Bronzeville. It could have been right next door to my old school Burke Elementary. What a jewel that would have been!

I spoke out forcefully and often, but in the end did not get my way—the Obama Presidential Center is being built in Jackson Park, closer to the lake and to the Apostolic Church of God. There were powerful forces that wanted it there. But at least it is coming to the South Side—hopefully with a Community Benefits Agreement—and I was very pleased to hear my voice on the video the Obama Foundation released to announce that it would be coming here. I believe that it will honor the great history here but be more than a museum—more of an active agent for social change, an agent that could also work to carry forward the legacy of Dr. King. Years from now, when I am no longer here to tell my stories, people will see that center and know what I was talking about. Only in Chicago. Only out of this Sacred Ground.

Maybe you can see why those tours around Bronzeville started taking on a more positive tone, a more forward-looking tone. Why my oral history interviews are, for all the troubles we face, sounding more hopeful. Yes, there is still a lot to overcome. But we have overcome a lot, and if we keep on keepin' on, this world will in the course of time belong to the People rather than the Establishment. All people are equal.

Epilogue:
The Future Belongs to Those
Who Fight for It

Lord, dear Lord above, God almighty,
God of love, please look down and see my people through.
I believe that God put sun and moon up in the sky.
I don't mind the gray skies
'cause they're just clouds passing by.

I wanted to use these words from the great Duke Ellington's lyric "Come Sunday" one more time, as I bring this story, the story of Sacred Ground, to a close. Whatever religious doubts I may have, I still sing these words to myself about every day. I do believe in "a brighter by and by" and "I don't mind the gray skies / 'cause they're just clouds passing by." Someone asked me: "What is your dominant emotion? Happiness? Anger? What?" I said right away, "Happiness, yes, gladness—gladness that I can still be here trying to make this world a better world." I think optimism has been a continuous feeling with me. I had my times of depression, serious depression during World War II and when my son died. I had so wanted him to carry on the torch. But overall my life has had a continuous feeling of optimism, that tomorrow is going to be a better day, that trouble don't last forever. This was how I carried on the legacy of my ancestors. My mama and daddy believed that tomorrow would be a better day, and my brother and I believed that too. Always. Still.

But again, I think that in many ways I am a typical person of my generation and my Sacred Ground. My story is one shared by so many of the others described in this book; I have tried, by sharing my experiences, to do justice to them too. To share the story of a community in a way that their children and children's children and children's children's children might hear and appreciate. They need to know that this Sacred Ground was what brought them the first black president of the United States. That we have done the impossible and maybe even the miraculous.

Yes, the struggle continues. It always seems to continue. But a century of experience has taught me that we can, together, continue it in a spirit of gladness and hope. May this be the prologue to your Sacred Ground.

Afterword:
Walking with My Father

Ermetra A. Black Thomas

A Touchstone and a Compass

In so many ways I am a fortunate person, but particularly in this regard: my father is an inspiring teacher. This should not be seen as an anomaly, as he was raised by teachers and in an environment where most adults felt and acted as if it was their God-given mission to mentor and teach each other and succeeding generations.

Dad's parents were witnesses to the aftermath of the destruction of the Civil War recovery acts of Abraham Lincoln—the Thirteenth, Fourteenth, and Fifteenth Amendments to the U.S. Constitution—and to the dismantling of the acts of postwar Reconstruction that led to Jim Crow. They were the children and grandchildren of the kidnapped and disempowered laborers who built many of the structures and much of the economy that has catapulted America to first-rank status across the globe. They taught by demonstrating their kindness and humor while passing on a mostly unwritten legacy through storytelling.

My father follows a tradition that shows what it knows. So he generally aims high and pushes the mission five or six steps beyond the expected. He taught my brother and me and many of his students with jocularity, stamina, and perseverance. Since the path usually was not paved smoothly, without bumps, he took some spills and lumps, yet endured and recovered. One of the salient lessons to me is that he, as was and is true of most men of color, is more hard-working, generous, and talented than most of those who oppose him.

And All That Jazz

Our home was filled with music. All kinds of music: Debussy, Ravel, Tchaikovsky, Beethoven, Bach, Fats Waller, Doris Day, Nat King Cole. For me, rites of passage were marked by the evolution of phonographic equipment: from chiming little Golden Records to 78 RPM European and popular classics; then Motown 45s and later LPs by Miles Davis, Peter, Paul and Mary, Pete Seeger, John Coltrane, Nina Simone, and Miriam Makeba. It was artistic expression and a valve to feel and see clearly. A lyrical songbook to right wrongs. These were my father's talking points. He could spin an exposition of epochs gone by listening to a riff by Duke Ellington or Johnny Hodges, or annotation by composer Billy Strayhorn. It inspired him, he tells us. It motivates and spurs us also.

Although I am not a musician, I have foundational memories of Saturdays riding with Dad on what is now called the Metra Electric—then popularly known as the IC (short for Illinois Central) to piano lessons at the Chicago Fine Arts Center. A treat of a five-cent Hershey's candy bar might follow. Again, I am not a talented singer or musician. But it was thanks to my father that I am a founding member of the Chicago Children's Choir, which began as the First Unitarian Church's junior choir—the brainchild of the late masterful and indefatigable Christopher Moore. The thread wove deeply as music became for me not only a marker of historical trends, but also a rhythmic lodestone to hear and understand other voices and to gather clues to discern and dissemble the unfamiliar or unknown-to-me aspects of life.

Walking Points and Appearances

Finally, I am fortunate to have started life in an era before driving a car was a necessity.

Therefore we walked, and talked while walking. This is how I learned the social and personal history of Chicago and of our family's travels and travails in the South (Birmingham and other regions of Alabama and Georgia) before their gathering in Chicago, Detroit, and then parts east to Connecticut and west to California, from my father, grandfather, and uncles during our journeys to museums and libraries, to Washington Park playgrounds for jungle gyms, teeter-totters, and swing sets, or to the Midway Plaisance for ice-skating or watching equestrians ride on horseback.

One excursion with my dad took me to a famous Hyde Park Baptist church where the poet Langston Hughes was speaking as a literary visitor from New York's Harlem. As a reader of his work, I was familiar with the author of Jess B. Semple's perorations. He loomed very large and tall in my imagination, but when I met the slight-but-average-proportioned poet, my instantaneous revelation was that Mr. Hughes, though still a hero in my mind's eye, was a normal human being—just like all of us.

Which brings me to the topic of appearance and countenance. Timuel Dixon Black Jr. is a cool and balanced individual. This is generally accepted. However, as a child, there was one moment when in a flash of recognition as one human glancing at another, I glimpsed something else in my father's face. I saw in him a handsome, striking, and noble person. Not just on the surface, but I realized with absolute certainty that there was a solid, luminous quality to his character. I saw this as an eight-year-old, and it's been a not very well kept secret ever since.

Recommended Reading

Black, Timuel D., Jr. *Bridges of Memory, Vol. 1: Chicago's First Wave of Black Migration*. Evanston, Ill., and Chicago: Northwestern University Press and DuSable Museum of African American History, 2005.

———. *Bridges of Memory, Vol. 2: Chicago's Second Generation of Black Migration*. Evanston, Ill., and Chicago: Northwestern University Press and DuSable Museum of African American History, 2007.

———. *The Timuel D. Black Jr. Papers, 1918–2010*. Vivian G. Harsh Research Collection of Afro-American History and Literature, Chicago Public Library, https://www.chipublib.org/fa-timuel-d-black-papers/.

Bone, Robert, and Richard A. Courage. *The Muse in Bronzeville: African American Creative Expression in Chicago, 1932–1950*. New Brunswick, N.J.: Rutgers University Press, 2011.

Finley, Marty Lou, Bernard LaFayette Jr., James R. Ralph Jr., and Pam Smith, eds. *The Chicago Freedom Movement: Martin Luther King Jr. and Civil Rights Activism in the North*. Lexington, Ky.: University Press of Kentucky, 2016.

Green, Adam. *Selling the Race: Culture, Community, and Black Chicago, 1940–1955*. Chicago: University of Chicago Press, 2007.

Helgeson, Jeffrey. *Crucibles of Black Empowerment: Chicago's Neighborhood Politics from the New Deal to Harold Washington*. Chicago: University of Chicago Press, 2014.

Herrick, Mary J. *The Chicago Schools: A Social and Political History*. New York: Sage Publications, 1970.

Holt, Thomas C. *Children of Fire: A History of African Americans*. New York: Hill and Wang, 2011.

Moore, Natalie Y. *The South Side: A Portrait of Chicago and American Segregation*. New York: St. Martin's Press, 2016.

Perkins, Useni Eugene. *Rise of the Phoenix: Voices from Chicago's Black Struggle, 1960–1975*. Chicago: Third World Press, 2017.

Schultz, Bart. *The Civic Knowledge Project Remembers 1942–43*. Chicago: University of Chicago Civic Knowledge Project video, 2008, http://humstatic.uchicago.edu/mahimahi/media/ckp/CKP-1942.mp4. See also the videos of the Professor Timuel D. Black Distinguished Guest Lecture and Jazz Concert series, available at http://civicknowledge.uchicago.edu/.

St. Clair Drake, John Gibbs. *Black Folk Here and There: An Essay in History and Anthropology*, 2 volumes. Los Angeles: Center for Afro-American Studies, 1987 and 1991.

———— and Horace Cayton. *Black Metropolis: A Study of Negro Life in a Northern City*. Chicago: University of Chicago Press, 1993 [1945].

Terkel, Studs. *The Good War: An Oral History of World War II*. New York: New Press, reprint ed. 1997.

Travis, Dempsey. *An Autobiography of Black Chicago*. Evanston, Ill.: Agate Bolden, rev. ed. 2014.

————. *Harold, The People's Mayor: The Biography of Harold Washington*. Evanston, Ill.: Agate Bolden, rev. ed. 2017.

Index

Chicago, *continued*
"plantation politics" of, 85–88;
Police Department, 72, 109, 128,
134; public libary system, 29;
public school system, 72, 85, 92,
96, 98, 109, 159; race riot (1919),
3; Robert Taylor Homes housing
project, 150; segregation in, 4;
sense of belonging in Chicago,
20–23; steel mills, 13, 15;
stockyards, 13, 15–16, 28; West
Side, 29, 82, 91, 100, 102, 108,
156. *See also* South Side
Chicago Bee Building, 155
Chicago Bee (newspaper), 5, 18
Chicago Children's Choir, 74, 166
Chicago Committee to Defend the
Bill of Rights, 110
Chicago Crusader (newspaper), 20
Chicago Daily News, 102
Chicago Defender (newspaper), 3,
18, 32, 102, 155; "Bud Billiken"
character, 27; "Come North,
young men" call of, 13; scandal
involving Rep. Powell, 86
Chicago Federation of Musicians
(CFM), 47
Chicago Fine Arts Center, 166
Chicago Freedom Movement, 84, 134
Chicago League of Negro Voters, 85,
96
Chicago Public Schools (CPS), 72,
85, 92, 96, 98, 109, 159
*Chicago Schools, The: A Social and
Political History* (Herrick), 91
Chicago Teachers Union, 77, 90
Chicago Urban League, 79, 80, 157
"Children of the Night" (T. K.
Black), 116
China, 4

churches, 3, 5, 33, 74, 75, 82; Bethel
Baptist Church (Birmingham),
75; First Unitarian Church of
Chicago, 74, 75, 166; Grant
Memorial Church, 105; Liberty
Baptist Church, 82, 84, 128, 156;
Olivet Baptist Church, 82; Quinn
Chapel A.M.E. Church, 33, 71;
St. Thomas Episcopal Church,
83; Tabernacle Missionary Baptist
Church, 128; Warren Avenue
Congregational Church, 82
City Colleges, 92, 98, 99, 113, 159
Civic Knowledge Project (CKP). *See
under* University of Chicago
civil rights movement, 9, 35, 69, 88,
104; generations of, 152; March
on Washington, 78–81, 98, 119,
140; Montgomery bus boycott,
147; in the North, 82; Obama
and legacy of, 145; sit-in tactic,
71, 91–92; taught in schools, 91–
92; unions and, 77. *See also* King,
Martin Luther, Jr.
Civil War recovery acts, 165
Clark, Irma, 124–25
Clark, Mark, 139
class conflict, 94, 95
Clifton, Nat "Sweetwater," 31
Clinton, Bill, 88
Clinton, Hillary, 145
Club DeLisa, 25
code-switching, 137, 138, 139
Cold War, 50
Cole, Nat King, 28, 30, 41, 42, 158, 166
Coleman, Bessie, 37
Coleman, Walter "Slim," 107
Colored Retail Clerks Union, 33
communism/communists (Reds), 26,
34, 36, 50, 79